THE BE

Vincent Mulchrone

A lifetime of wit and

observation of the folly

and splendour of his

fellow humans by the

Daily Mail's

finest reporter.

Revel Barker
Publishing

This edition published in Great Britain by Revel Barker Publishing, 66 Florence Road, Brighton BN1 6DJ

revelbarker@gmail.com

CONTENTS

Vincent Mulchrone

by

Vere Harmsworth

VINCENT MULCHRONE spent almost all his professional life on the *Daily Mail* but there was hardly a newspaper in Fleet Street which did not print an appreciation of him or which was not represented at his funeral by fellow journalists – and rivals – who were his friends. He had no enemies. It is hard to think of a journalist whose death would bring such an overwhelming and personal response, from Buckingham Palace and *The Times* to the *Morley Observer* and the *Suffolk Free Press.* Letters poured into the *Daily Mail,* whose columns he lit up for nearly thirty years, from readers who thought of him as their friend in print and to all those who knew and loved him personally in Yorkshire, in Ireland and in journalism the world over. There was no envy in journalists' admiration for Vincent. They knew he was a great reporter. They took pleasure in his pleasure in what magic can be made with the English language, in spite of the hurdles and the deadlines that newspapers impose.

His gifts were humour and humanity relieved by a certain sharpness, even acidity, which restrained his writing from being sentimental. He delighted in people of every kind except the pompous and the self-important, to whom he could be merciless.

He loved human foibles, the contrariness of the rural Irish, for example, and the earthy realism of Yorkshire's industrial West Riding, both of which he combined in his own character. He loved the weird saga of the giant Denby Dale pie, or the customers who bought the local in their Irish village rather than let it be changed by a stranger, or the Pakistani immigrant on Skye who was more Gaelic than the Scots. He was pleased at being a fairly terrible golfer – his ambition he said was a handicap of 16 and a waistline twice as much. He regarded golf as an excuse for a long walk with a friend.

With all his personal magnetism, which caused people to gather round him in any bar, he was modest, gentle and brave. His modesty made him uneasy when paid a compliment, because his work, however brilliant, never quite satisfied him. He was gentle and unfailingly courteous to the people whose triumphs or disasters he reported and he was always ready to help a less experienced reporter competing in covering the same story. His bravery was deeply hidden by his humour. After serving in one war as an RAF pilot, he covered other wars as human events. When his illness struck him, he said to a close friend: 'I know what it is, but I don't want to know when.' He was too polite, too sensitive to embarrassment ever to refer to it among his colleagues.

Vincent will always be remembered as a writer who did more to popularise the Royal Family than a hundred purveyors of sycophantic prose. On royal travels and state occasions his eye was alert not for the pomp and ceremony but for human detail. He liked them as human beings, as well as admiring them as professionals who did a taxing job with style and dedication, and he wanted others to share that knowledge. He once devoted 1,000 words to a royal ticking off for Prince Philip. He explained why he had such a reputation for abrasiveness with the Press and advised him: 'Stay as sweet as you are – and just as difficult,' adding: 'Why should he change? We won't.'

Perhaps his favourite story of unpompous royal behaviour was the royal cocktail party for the Press at which a photographer, seeing the Queen coming to talk to him, dropped his glass on the carpet and later, when it was time to take the pictures, found that again and again his flash failed to go off. 'Just not your day, is it, Mr Reed?' murmured the Queen as she swept regally past. There was also an opening of the Ideal Home Exhibition by Princess Alexandra, at which Vincent found himself being passed a brightly coloured plastic brush which had been presented to the Princess by an eager exhibitor as an unscheduled gift. Months later at a palace party, she asked him with a smile if he'd still got the brush. Why, he asked, would she like it back?

He felt in some ways, paradoxically, that he was a failure as a writer because he confined his talents to daily journalism, which is read, crumpled up and thrown away. It did not occur to him that what he achieved could only be accumulated over the years through daily written journalism, a more direct and immediate communication from writer to reader than either books, on one hand, or television, on the other. He took tremendous pride in his craft but he simply did not know how good he was.

He could penetrate in a flash to the heart of a story in a few deceptively simple words. He wrote of Churchill's lying-in-state beside the Thames at Westminster Hall: 'Two rivers run through London tonight and one of them is made of people.' When objects were thrown at the Queen's car in Ulster he wrote: 'A breeze block and a bottle of stout were flung into Irish history here today.'

He loved what he called 'the most exciting trade in the world.' When he won one of his awards as a descriptive writer, he wrote, 'Journalism, like war, is 90 per cent sitting on someone else's laurels and the rest sheer panic. If, in the panic, you can find words to convey the blood and sweat of the revolution in Oojiboo and, which is frequently more difficult, get them back to a sub-editor who is worried about his train home to Orpington, then you are a reporter and the happiest animal on earth.' He asked to be remembered, not with miserable faces but with joy, and he deserves that joy as our thanks for having known him and read him.

The man
I sat beside

'I, and the best pork pies in the world, come from Morley,' Vincent claimed with Yorkshire pride. He was born there in 1923, grew up in a modest street of terraced houses, left the local grammar school at 16 and, after an interlude dressing window dummies and driving a lemonade lorry, joined the local paper, the 'Morley Observer'. His debut as a reporter was swiftly interrupted by his war service as a pilot, which took him to Java.

He joined the Daily Mail in 1950 in Manchester, moving to Fleet Street in 1954, becoming head of the Paris Bureau in 1957 and then settling into his natural vocation as a feature writer and special reporter, for which he won awards as Descriptive Writer of the Year (1964) and Feature Writer of the Year (1970). On the way he married his Ulster-born wife, Louie, on whom he utterly relied. His three sons, Martin, Patrick and Michael, were his pride and their family life was his very private retreat between the bouts of globe-trotting that made him the paper's most travelled and most admired writer.

The extra demand that newspaper work makes on a writer of quality is that he knows his first hundred words count double. The first hundred Vincent dealt you always made you sit up and go on reading. He always, when I sat beside him, wrote his 'intros' in pencil, screwing up sheets of paper until the words gave off an exciting fizz – like the sound of the foam when the first wave runs up the dry sand.

He wrote some of his best pieces in the journalist's familiar conditions of heat, haste and exhaustion at the end of a frustrating, perhaps dangerous, journey, in a cable office staffed by an operator who speaks no English. The following pages are only a taste of his quality. So much of his prose is timeless, full of acute perception of the quirks of humanity that he savoured. The tragedy is that, when leukaemia struck him down at the age of 54, he had so much more in him to write – and there is no one else who could write it in the way he would have done.

PETER LEWIS

REPORTER AT LARGE

The witness of a cake of soap

Jerusalem 1961: The world was waiting for Adolf Eichmann, after his abduction from South America, to stand in the dock.

BY CANDLELIGHT in a cellar on Mount Zion today a young Jew and I gazed for a long time at a cake of yellow soap. Said the Jew: 'The thing you will never be able to understand is that that might have been made from my uncle.'

I was reminded for a moment of the most devilish cruelty ever perpetrated on man. And that cake of soap, made from the fat of a Jew by the Nazis, will play its hidden part in the Eichmann trial simply by being here on Mount Zion. To see the revolting object is to understand all the high charged emotion which swirls around the stage being readied for the Eichmann drama.

To get to the soap you climb Mount Zion under the eyes of Israeli sentries. They loll behind their sandbags, high in the tower of the Church of the Dormition where Mary, the mother of Jesus, died. You bypass the tomb of David and pass through dark vaults where squatting Jews light candles for their dead. And there is what they call 'The Chamber of Destruction.' There, in the flickering candlelight, is the soap.

It stands on top of a glass jar, half-full of deadly pellets of 'cyclone B,' the gas which killed Jews by the million in Auschwitz and other extermination camps. A sign reads: 'We won't forget the blood – and the Lord rests in Zion.'

In glass cases rests more evidence of inhumanity and degradation, carefully preserved from the concentration camps – the sacred parchments of the Torah made into tambourines, wallets and even shoes. It is as though a conqueror of Christians had fashioned a sacred communion wafer into a ludo counter. Some of the Torahs are smeared with the blood of those who died holding them.

There is an air of unspeakable death and degradation about the place, and the candles do not relieve the chill. There are the ashes too – dozens of attractive blue and white-striped jars containing the mortal remains of a selection of the 6,000,000 Jews slaughtered by the Nazis.

These ashes, in the cases ironically supporting the poison-gas pellets and the soap, will bring the Eichmann trial to a halt on Wednesday evening. The trial, and everything else in Israel, will be brought to a halt by a day of mourning for these ashes – 'Memorial Day for the victims of the holocaust.' From the death chamber on Mount Zion a portion of the ashes, representing just one of the thousands of annihilated Jewish communities of Europe, will be borne to a new resting place on Mount Hertzl, on the other side of the new city.

It is just a coincidence that the newly instituted Holocaust Day interrupts the Eichmann trial almost before it has properly begun. But it is a coincidence which bodes no good for Eichmann. The ex-SS lieut-colonel who was the chief bureaucrat of the butchery of the Jews is somewhere above my head at the moment, high in the new community building which will be the scene of his trial. If he can see out from his bare room on the top floor he will see a familiar sight – Jews standing behind a wire fence – their hands clinging to the strands. Only, this time, the Jews are on the outside of the wire.

I was thoroughly searched before being allowed into the 250-seat Press room beneath the court today. Every article of equipment coming through the gun-guarded gates was minutely examined for hidden arms or bombs. Eichmann, for the moment at least, is the safest man in Israel.

Today they put the finishing touches to his glass-encased dock, a fish-tank sort of a structure which reminds me irresistibly of that in which the Rector of Stiffkey fasted (for 6d a look) on Blackpool's Golden Mile before the war. So there sits Eichmann thinking heaven knows what thoughts, high above the sun-drenched streets of Jerusalem. His chief judge sits at home, very probably playing the piano. Supreme Court Judge Moshe Landau has been refusing all invitations to dinner with friends in case the trial should be mentioned in his hearing. He is a fine pianist and in recent days has spent many hours playing all by himself.

Some of Eichmann's enemies are sunning themselves by their picnic baskets on Mount Zion – within revolver shot of Jordan's wary border on the Old City Wall and within wailing distance of that cake of soap which assuredly was somebody's uncle.

Horribly, though without much malice, the native-born Israeli sometimes calls a Jew who survived Hitler's persecution 'soap'. Tough and uncompromising, they cannot understand how so many European Jews, as though hypnotised by the Nazi snake, gave themselves almost without protest to the gas chambers. But in Jerusalem tonight 'soap' is not a bad word. That little yellow block of obscene fat on Mount Zion is about to take its revenge on Adolf Eichmann.

11 April 1961

The lonely monster in a new blue suit

AS THE BELLS of Jerusalem rang nine today the Jews offered their prisoner to the sight of the world – a desperately lonely, balding monster who has a new suit and a cold in the head. The local tailor who made the suit specially for Adolf Eichmann did not, perhaps, put his best skill into it.

It would never pass the inspection of a Jewish tailor in Leeds, and it has not yet had time to settle into the folds of Eichmann's body. So it heightens the impression of stiffness as the prisoner stands to hear the long litany of horror which is the indictment.

Still, it is a good enough dark-blue suit. And, anyway, very few people here expect that he'll be wearing it long.

Everything about him, as we should have known, is an anticlimax. There never was a murderer who stepped into the dock at the Old Bailey without people saying: 'Do you mean to say that little runt killed all those women?'

So it is with Eichmann.

Murder, when done in a moment and singly in a dark lane, or over years and to millions in the broad daylight of history, leaves no mark on the killer's face. Eichmann's face shows nothing but self-control and occasionally, when told to stand or sit or put on his earphones, a quick expression which shows a desire to please, to be 'Korrect'.

He looks Jewish, of course – far more Jewish than any of the blonde or red-headed Jews in the courtroom, Jews who give him a look which is thousands of years old. The hook-nose (subject of taunts when he was a child and the reason, perhaps, for heaven knows what deadly complexes later) was untouched by plastic surgery in his years in hiding.

His baldness follows the usual pattern. A neat tonsure with a little fuzz, a combs-breadth of dark hair swept carefully across the top, and a high, shiny forehead which, together with the aquiline face, gives an impression of sharp intelligence. The man looks like a thoughtful senior bureaucrat. Which is just what he was.

'I'm afraid we'll have to work late again tonight, Miss Schultz, Herr Himmler wants another 10,000 to be processed for Auschwitz. I don't know *where* we'll find the transport.

'Yes, in triplicate, please. And we must tell Hoess to make a neater job of the gold teeth this time. Yes, please. But with two lumps this time.'

What, *that* little man in that glass box – *he* sent all those millions to their deaths? Yes, that little man, that ordinary looking little man. That not-a-bit-sorry-looking little man who, when he forgets, kneads his right thumb into the back of his left hand. 'Beautiful hands,' said a Jewess at my side. Then she gave a little nervous giggle.

Only the mouth is what you would expect – and only then because of the Gestapo image created in the cinema. It is a thin, compressed slit set in sallow flesh, and it turns down at the ends. It could be a brutal mouth or merely a strong mouth, depending on how you feel about its owner. But that's all.

He is Adolf Eichmann. He is the greatest killer unhung. He is in the tightest corner in the world. Yet he looks much like any other man, and your attention wanders from him.

Even the Jews, who in a sense have waited centuries for this moment, find you can't go on looking forever at something which turns out to be just another man.

Now the great businesslike propaganda set-piece is ready to claim the attention of the world. In the clattering word-factory beneath the courtroom 400 newspaper and television men are snatching a last cigarette and hanging transistor radio receivers and earphones (£12. 10s. deposit) round their necks. On Channel Four you can hear a simultaneous English translation of the wrath of the Jews in Hebrew and the answers of the defence in German. You move, and transistors make the story of bestiality portable. Volume strength three will do for the courtroom. You need strength four in the bar, five in the restaurant across the way. In the basement lavatories, words like Lidice and torture and genocide fade away almost forgotten, so nobody wastes much time there.

On the closed-circuit television screens the credit titles come up – *'The Trial of Adolf Eichmann.* Produced by Milton A Fruchtman: A Capital Cities Production.' This New York TV company has sole rights and is selling its video tape round the world. The proceeds to charity. Four hidden cameras, shooting through holes in the auditorium walls, stare long at Eichmann, get bored, range along the judges bench, pick up a furiously scribbling reporter in the stalls, then cut again to Eichmann.

Still photographs, taken by Government photographers in court, are quickly processed and sold at 10s. a time, to a crowd of pleading photographers in the Press room who then race 20 yards to the counter from where they will be radioed round the world. And all the time a clattering cacophony of typewriters (the Israeli ones working, hypnotically, backwards) are spewing the story the Jews insist has never been fully told.

The blue strip-lighting above the stage – for it really is a stage they all sit on here in the new community centre – drops a bright pinpoint of light on the noble bald head of Presiding Judge Moshe Landau.

There is a little flash of white, and Eichmann is dabbing at his sniffles with an advert-bright handkerchief. Such a human thing, the sniffles. Some of them probably had the sniffles when they stepped down into their mass graves. But, being naked, they couldn't have handkerchiefs.

Judge Landau causes some surprise by reading the Attorney-General's indictment himself.

Through the guttural sonorous Hebrew come sounds one can recognise – Geshtapo, Berleen, Auschwitz, der millione Yehudim... with the German translation it takes 75 minutes, and Eichmann stands throughout.

'Never moved a muscle – I'll give him that,' said someone.

Eichmann spoke only twice: 'Are you Adolf Eichmann?' he was asked; and 'Did you understand the indictment?' We saw, rather than heard, the 'Jawohl'.

Then the lawyers took over – Jewish lawyers arguing before Jewish judges in the Jewish capital – the right of the Jews to try their great decimator. A slight unreality began to creep in. Grizzled, grey-haired defence counsel, Dr Robert Servatius challenged the right in German. All three judges are German-born. German was their first tongue. But before they could officially 'hear' Dr Servatius they had to wait for his words to be translated into Hebrew (and more than once Judge Landau expertly corrected his translator's translation). And every time the Presiding Judge wanted to interrupt the flow of the German lawyer he used the English words 'one moment', which can sound surprisingly cutting.

All day (except for an hour in which the entire Israeli court went to the funeral of a colleague) the legal argument was tossed back and forth: 'This court has not the right,' says the German. 'Oh, yes it has,' says the Israeli. 'Can the judges rise above prejudice?' asks the German. 'Certainly,' says the Israeli. 'This is revenge,' says the German. 'This is justice,' says the Jew.

Words like 'expiation' and 'reparation' and 'slaughter' and 'kidnapped' drift unreally on the transistor-geared radio waves, and Eichmann, settled comfortably in his chair, becomes a cipher, a great irrelevance.

He sits with his head poked to one side, eyes fixed on the judges, never looking at us. Sometimes he moistens his lips.

Both movements, at times, have been known to suggest guilt. But not here. Eichmann doesn't *look* guilty. But then that, perhaps, would be too much to expect.

12 April 1961

The Wolf of Kabul comes home at last

WHEN FIRST I DEFENDED THE KHYBER single handed against the King's enemies I had to make do with the Wesleyan Chapel graveyard for Afghan territory and the roof of our dustbin shed for the beleaguered fort at Landi Kotal. Still, I was the Wolf of Kabul and the Raj was safe at least until bedtime.

CHAPTER ONE

The fantasy was lifted straight from my weekly comic. The Wolf of Kabul was, of course, a British agent cunningly rigged out as a Pathan. His faithful Afridi servant carried as a weapon a huge cricket bat, bound about with wire, which he called 'clicky-ba'. And never a bearded stranger with snow on his boots entered the Khyber from the north without the Wolf of Kabul being ready for him.

Oh, the Russians I've picked off from that dustbin shed.

And now, 30 years later, the reality.

And at first sight, no surprise. If you know the colours of the workaday West Riding – mill chimney black, chapel roof grey, industrial effluent brown – you know the colours on a winter's day of the Khyber Pass. The rainclouds are as threatening, the wind as keen, and the great waterfalls of scree are the shape and colour of pit tips.

Then, to interrupt the unromantic reveries, three men come loping down the precipitous road. They are Maridis, tall and rugged and fair of skin, and every man with a rifle slung on his shoulder. And suddenly you feel the thrill of the Khyber, the most fabled, bloodstained gateway of Asia, the hard-won farthermost limit of the British Raj.

It is only rarely nowadays that blood feuds between the tribesmen are settled with guns. But, rather like a City gent carrying an umbrella in summer, the Afridis and Shinwaris, the Shilimanies and the Mullagories work on the principle 'You never know,' and seldom leave their front door without a firearm. Almost every dark little shop has a box of cartridges at its doorway – an after-thought department rather like the chocolate stall of a self-service store. *('Oh, yes, I forgot the old man wanted a dozen rounds of 303's.')*

For these proud, independent hillmen the self-protection habit is based on sound, historic reason. They have been ready for trouble ever since the 5th Century BC, when Darius the Persian led his armies through the pass to the plains of the Indus. Alexander's soldiers slaughtered and raped here. So did the hordes of Genghis Khan and Timurlane, Babar and Nadir Shah, who, when he returned through the pass, carried £30,000,000-worth of loot from Delhi. And £30,000,000 bought a lot of dancing girls in 1738.

The fort where I am writing this probably has memories for a young subaltern who had to fight his way here when the Afridis seized the Khyber in 1897. They told me his name. Winston Churchill, or something like that.

Here the Queen will lunch tomorrow in the mess of the Khyber Rifles, latest of a long line of guardians of the Pass. Previous guardians left behind their regimental crests carved in the rock.

The Wolf of Kabul was home at last. But the Rifles' adjutant, Major Yaqub Gul, proved a disappointment to an old Khyber hand like myself. 'Most peaceful place on earth nowadays,' he said. 'The tribesmen are turning into technicians and traders and contractors. They're working as miners and masons on the new Warsak Dam. Their children are going to school and some even to university down in Peshawar and the older people are very proud of them.

'Why, when they go down to Peshawar nowadays they even leave their rifles at home.'

From the fort walls I looked back along the pass, over the hilltop blockhouses with which we finally overcame the tribesmen, to the green plains where the Queen has achieved a different sort of conquest in the past fortnight.

And there's no shadow of doubt about it, she has captured their republican hearts down there on the plains of India and Pakistan. The thousands on the roof tops along every royal route will take a lot of forgetting. And there were the villagers who stuck Union Jacks in the nosebands of their camels. And when you asked them why they said simply: 'For the Queen.'

Above all there was my friend the ex-terrorist, drinking rum in a Delhi club and insisting, 'We never at any time hated the British. That's why the whole keynote of this tour is going to be affection. We like the Queen because she represents you. And we like you.'

These are very moving memories to be savouring here high in the Khyber. And I would savour them longer if the Khyber wasn't so cold. Did I say cold? At the Khyber Rifles mess the waiters wore greatcoats and wool caps.

I didn't. Which is why the Wolf of Kabul is about to tuck himself up in beddibyes with two aspirins and a glass of amber liquid which has successfully made the journey from a faraway land.

Oh, well, the dream had to end somewhere.

6 February 1961

Solved: The mystery of Mademoiselle from Armentieres

WHEN THE POOR BUT HONEST DIE, all that remains personal to them can be – and with weird frequency is – contained in a cardboard shoe box. And it was no different with the Mademoiselle from Armentieres.

With almost a million dead soldiers looking over my shoulder I emptied her shoe box today. There wasn't much. A formal studio portrait, balancing her little daughter on a table. Her pension book. The dramatic red card which suggested that as she had been touched by war (more particularly, by German mustard gas) you might have the decency to give her your seat in the train.

The photograph stuck, as the law demands, on the top right-hand corner of the card, shows a dark, angular face with tight lips. It's odd to think that this was the last woman's face those to die saw… serving beer in the Café de la Paix. From the cafe they turned left to the station, then left again for the Front and, two miles later, they were with their Maker.

Some of them went to their deaths singing bawdy verses about her. Which is odd, in a way, for she was a most proper woman. And odder still, in another way, is the fact that until today, Armentieres had no idea who she was. I, with due deference, told them.

She was, to put the record straight once and for all, Marie Lecocq. She was born at precisely 10am on August 8, 1890, to an Armentieres sand merchant and his Belgian wife in the Rue Solferino.

Until his dying day, nine years ago, the British soldier who wrote the song about her did not know that she was, at the time he wrote it, a widow. It should have been (though it wouldn't have scanned, of course) *Madame* from Armentieres.

Mademoiselle's ghost (against which her marital status at the time is nothing) has been called from the shadows by the brighter sparks of Armentieres who felt, in the words of one of them, that they have been neglecting a ready-made heroine. They know that the song – second only, perhaps, to *Tipperary* in evocative appeal – will be 50 years old next spring. It is then that they will unveil a statue to Mademoiselle, a stylised wraith (according to preliminary drawings) supported by four soldiers – a Tommy, a kilted Scot, an Anzac and an Indian.

The notion gains charm because Armentieres is a sort of Halifax of the Nord, all terrace houses and textiles and engineering, and chips and peas, and the Rotary meets on Monday.

Last January, Armentieres asked every French Consul in every English-speaking country in the world to spread the idea and ask for donations. The result has astonished even the most optimistic of the committee of 30. They have had £2 from a lady in Hamilton, Lanarkshire, ten bob from a veteran in Doncaster, a quid (Australian) from New South Wales.

Most of the letters are in the spidery writing of old men or old widows. Most of the old men claim they *knew* Mademoiselle from Armentieres. And some of the widows claim they *are*.

The letters, the donations, the claims of the aged pretenders, lie on the desk of M. Antoine Debosque in the office behind his antique shop on the square. He is 65, an Anglophile, a wit. And he was, this morning, confused.

'We have come to the conclusion,' he said, 'that she must have been a myth.' But she was not. Before he died Edward Rowland typed out the story of how he came to write the song. And he talked about Mademoiselle.

She was Marie Lecocq, he said. She served in the Café de la Paix, in the Rue de la Gare. She was neat and clean and polite, and it stuck in his mind that she would break off serving drinks to officers to make coffee for the boys. 'The real Mademoiselle from Armentieres,' he said, 'was very strait-laced and stood no nonsense from the troops... not at all the sort of girl some of the lurid, parodied versions invented by the troops later made her out to be...' I think it was this that made M. Debosque sit up. 'Exactly her,' he said. 'Every letter I have says just this.'

The song itself? According to the composer, then a 27-year-old Service Corps sergeant, he was in the Café de la Paix the day Marie slapped the face of an officer who tried to take a liberty. He wrote his song, and that night sang all three verses. Later he wrote another 120. He also wrote, in later years, a vital clue. Marie, he said, was waiting to marry a local man called Marceau.

M. Debosque and I almost ran across the square to the Town Hall. The French registry of births, marriages and deaths must be one of the world's most efficient.

CHAPTER ONE

There she was, in faded ink, Marie Lecocq, who married, first, in 1909, Maurice Bintein; in August 1915 (five months after the face-slap and the song) Julien Vandewalle; and, in 1926, Marceau Gisquiere. She died at Marquette, on the outskirts of nearby Lille, on January 19, 1945. Unmourned, save by her family. Unsung by the troops.

But by Vandewalle she had a daughter. 'Yes, Monsieur, she is still alive. She is now, let's see, the widow Candry, 24, Rue de la Victoire.' And at Rue de la Victoire the widow Candry said: 'Yes, Messieurs, I am the daughter of Mademoiselle from Armentieres. Please come in.'

She produced the shoe box. She was cleaning for her youngest's First Communion on Sunday so, please, no photographs.

No, her mother had never sung the song, though sometimes she talked about slapping the officer's face.

'Whenever people have talked about Mademoiselle from Armentieres I have kept quiet about it – you understand? She was a good woman. She would give you the chemise from her back – and often did.'

Mademoiselle has a granddaughter, Marie-Therese, a winning blonde who works at a brewery in Lille, and, through her, even a great-grandson, Didier.

The Café de la Paix is one of the few buildings in Armentieres which survived the bombardments of both world wars. But two years ago, it closed its doors and hasn't opened them since.

There, for a few minutes today, I tried to visualise the Mademoiselle. And failed. Then M. Debosque and I went to the cemetery and found her grave. She lies for all time with Marceau in a plot not half so grand as those of granite and black mourning marble afforded by Alfred Buseyne, on her right, or Albert Tricot, on her left.

The sun, by this time, was going down over the graves of the war dead. 'There you are, M. Debosque,' I said. *'There's* Mademoiselle from Armentieres.'

Thank you, M. Mulchrone,' he replied. And he was rather sad.

'No, thank *you,* M. Debosque.'

And I was sad, too.

16 May 1964

Nehru finally quit the stage he had dominated so long

PANDIT NEHRU was most lovingly burned to ashes by his grandson this evening. Sanjay Gandhi, aged 18, put a match to camphor. Camphor sparked ghee, ghee burned sawdust, sawdust spread fire to sandalwood logs and the logs mingled their ashes with those of a man who, until two days ago, was the leader and inspiration of 460 million people, the inspiration of the modern Commonwealth and the last demi-god in the fabulous story called India.

From a crowd that could be measured only in square miles came cries of 'He is immortal' when his mortal remains were laid, uncoffined, on a piece of waste land by the bank of the Jumna River which is soon to be a children's playground.

He lay with his head to the right, as though that famous profile was taking a last look at the Old Red Fort. At his feet (and though it was a mile away it was still covered by the same crowd) was the spot where he himself had put the torch to Mahatma Gandhi's wasted little body in 1948. On that occasion he kissed the dead feet of his master. Today his own were kissed by his grandson, another Gandhi, though no relation to the Mahatma.

As priests raised a high nasal chant of prayers for the dead and the reincarnation to come the boy helped their assistants to stack the logs around and over Mr Nehru's body. It happened on a hastily built brick platform, 15ft square and 4ft high on which everyone went about barefoot on petals. Mr Nehru's flag-covered body, stretcher-borne by six senior officers, was laid gently on a structure in which wood was already stacked.

More gently still, the boy began to lay smooth 20in. logs on his grandfather's body. He laid them up to his chin. There he stopped. He had tied a white handkerchief round his forehead to stop perspiration running into his eyes as he went about the grim work. But he had to wipe his forehead. Mr Nehru's bald head, the great forehead, eyes and hooked nose, were still visible – and watched with fascinated intensity by those whose rank or position gave them a vantage point. It was the last anyone would see of a man many times larger than life.

The bustle on the platform was stilled and the hush spread. The moment was too much for Mr Nehru's sister, Madame Pandit. She turned away and began blindly to push her way towards the steps. The priest's assistants, seeing that the grandson made no move to complete the task, gently placed three logs across the proud face. And he was gone.

Anointed with a sandalwood extract, sprinkled with water from the sacred Ganges, wrapped in white silk, Mr Nehru finally quit the stage he had dominated for so long.

For all his simplicities he had loved a show as dearly as he loved people, and his going would have been very much to his taste, for it was both spectacular and moving. *He* went to his funeral pyre through the streets of Delhi borne high on a gun-carriage. He looked like an old man peacefully asleep in bed. Since his death he had lain like that in his own porch, his head cradled comfortably in a large white pillow and tipped higher than his feet, the better to be seen by the never-ending stream of mourners – bristling Rajputs and Dogras and Gurkhas, who threw him up a smart one as they passed, careworn old women from the countryside, who had put their hands together in a prayerful 'Namaste' as they gaped at him lying there beneath a patchwork quilt of exotic blooms.

A little after noon today they exchanged the flowers for the Indian flag and laid the corpse, still tipped head high, on to the gun-carriage. And they gave him a head-board covered with deep crimson bougainvillea. It was not his favourite flower. That was the English rose, which he invariably wore in a buttonhole of his long-skirted black achkan. And the last of those that his body passed today was the favourite he planted himself by his front steps – the little yellow McGredy's Sunset.

Lady Pamela Hicks brought him roses early today. She was Nehru's pet. With her father, Earl Mountbatten, she flew here through the night in Sir Alec Douglas-Home's plane. And she and Lord Louis paused only to change before going to see the man whose life had been so deeply interwoven with theirs. The last Viceroy brought a wreath.

Lady Pamela wept. And women in the crowd wept when the old statesman, riding high in his last bed, was drawn by 60 other ranks through his gates. The sun was a brazen, brutal thing building up to a temperature of 110 degrees, and the crowds had neither eaten nor supped since they formed at dawn – for, in contrast to Gandhi's funeral, neither hawkers of sweetmeats nor water sellers would work today.

The statesman's last journey was also his greatest. Estimates of the crowd vary from one and a half to three million. But it was one of those throngs beyond estimation, for crowds like that rarely happen. It was the biggest they had ever encountered said the police, bigger by far than that at Gandhi's funeral.

It was an Indian crowd, of course, rich in variety and excitement, with startling glimpses of wild-haired holy men, women of great caste and beauty, sightless wretches and holy cows. The onlookers were in every tree, on every rooftop, and the brass-tipped lathis of the police flickered discouragingly about the front rank whenever it seemed ready to break.

The crowd cried blessings on 'Chacha' (Uncle) Nehru, or called on heaven and each other to witness his obvious immortality. Muffled drums beat a path for him and poor people scattered petals and sometimes the leafy branches they had broken from the trees to give themselves a little portable shade. He passed the proud pink palace which Lutyens conceived for the Raj and where Nehru was later to show the military splendour of independent India to the Queen whose Commonwealth he helped to reshape.

The Raj Path, Delhi's massive processional way, was a sea, a mighty ocean of people. He passed the statue of King George V, orb and sceptre still in hand, now a grandstand for the mourners of the great republican. He left the magnificent avenues for ways where the pavements petered out and where hundreds of thousands of following feet raised the dust fine as skin-tinted talc and obscured the front of the cortege from the rear.

From the ramparts of the old city forts, from high perches in the eucalyptus trees, the people shouted their goodbyes. And when the procession came to the open ground near the Jumna the following thousands fanned out in a great swarm which covered the entire landscape. To cover six miles through those crowds had taken three hours. The Service chiefs lifted their precious burden from the gun carriage and carried it through the strangely quiet crowd.

The tall grandson, rushed back from a mountaineering holiday in Kashmir for his unenviable task, went ahead with his mother, Mrs Indira Gandhi. The great men of the Congress, Nehru's successor among them – but who? – crowded on to the platform to look just once more.

There was a ragged volley, a 'Last Post' that rang clear to the Red Fort. Then there were only the flames, and those very close to the man inside them who were given the privilege of adding a small piece of wood to the fire. And one of the last fell very gently from the hand of the last Viceroy.

29 May 1964

21

CHAPTER ONE

Down among the toy men

IN THE DEPARTURE LOUNGE of Tokio's modern international airport a motor-cycle cop ran across a British passenger's foot, stopped his bike, got off, remounted, and roared away. 'Amazing,' said the Briton, and bought the motor-bike, complete with cop, for 15s. 6d.

Before he had time to put his wallet away he spotted another of Japan's incredible toys. This one was a bear, a comfortable old Bruin in sports jacket and slippers, who walked at the touch of a button. As he walked he raised his pipe to his lips. The pipe bowl glowed hotly. Uncle Bruin took the pipe from his lips, walked a few steps more, then puffed out a cloud of smoke.

His toping cousin on the counter ambled along with a glass in one hand, a bottle in the other. Every few steps he poured himself a drink. He raised the glass to his lips and poured the quite real liquid down his throat.

Both Bruins were the same price, 15s. We were going to buy them for our children back in London. Until we discovered the telephones. Two telephones in pale blue plastic, each with a button which rings a bell on the other hand-set.

To me they seemed rather expensive at 35s., until I discovered the secret. They work with the aid of miniature transistors. You can communicate along the 20 yards of flex provided.

I have never seen such wonderful toys in my life. Never again will anybody sell me the story of little yellow men sneaking around English toy fairs trying to copy our designs.

For any little yellow men interested I have in my home, a super plastic English six-shooter which breaks every time you whip it from the holster. The holster is coming apart too.

11 April 1959

22

A mountain tired and shrugged a town off its shoulder

WHEN DAWN DIMMED the fairylights strung among the conifers in the little municipal park it seemed as if the flower beds were stirring. But the strengthening light showed them to be beds of people, the green their blankets and the red their blood.

Their cots were packed tight along every path. As they stirred in the chill air old men bustled to bring them tiny glasses of tea and nurses, grey-faced with fatigue, peeled at layers of blood-stained bandages.

An air of unreality lingers about earthquake towns long after the first incredible shock. Here it lies in the fairylights twinkling on a tatty triumphal arch, a sort of halo over the injured. The arch is only plywood. The quake failed to budge it, though it sliced the fronts off half a dozen stout shops nearby like a circular saw going through a layer cake.

Yet Gonabad, headquarters of Iran's earthquake rescue operations, counts itself lucky to have only a handful of dead, 600 injured, and pleasant parks for the less seriously injured to sleep in. But half an hour away from here the horror would almost choke you.

Across an arid, burning plain saw-toothed mountains rise. The village has clung to the lower slopes for centuries, and the mountain has sheltered it from sun and wind and given it water. And from the plain today it looked as it always did – from a distance that is. As in some scene from a Biblical calendar the herdsmen were tending their black goats and wizened sheep – the animals have the best survival rate here – outside the lushness of the village.

The dome of the mosque glows turquoise in the early light and shady trees still line the streets. The rest is a pile of mud, or rather hundreds of piles of mud, like so many ant heaps with groups of human beings working

23

atop each. But where nobody is working there are no survivors. I watched whole families, fully 20ft above ground level, arguing where the walls used to be so as to know where to start digging for their possessions. Six thousand people lived here. Little more than 2,000 remain, and scores of those are orphans who ran away on to the plain at the very sight of their dead parents.

This is Kakhk. A few days ago the mountain apparently tired of the little town and simply shrugged it off its shoulder.

In Kakhk they don't know what epicentre means. But they have a terrible intimacy with death. They are burying their dead still as the gravely injured die.

I watched a man carry his infant son to the graveyard, which has expanded fourfold overnight. The little corpse was tightly swaddled in muslin. The father carried it through the village streets in the nearest thing to hand, which happened to be the kind of tray the sweetmeat man uses to carry sticky buns. He cried noisily as he walked. His wife, veiled and silent, followed directly behind him. A cloud of flies followed both.

On the kerb a bundle of rags stirred and turned into an incredibly old woman, a widow they said. She took not the least notice of the funeral procession. She was kneeling, resting her weight on her elbows. She had a bundle, a kettle and cup from which she was drinking tea. Flies settled on the rim of the cup under her nose. She was either too weary, or too unconcerned, to shoo them off.

It is easy to see why the village's death roll is so startlingly high. The immensely thick mud brick walls had been added to by the generations. Some fell on people taking their siesta. And some of the slabs weigh several tons.

Sometimes a bit of the first floor held and debris from the roof trapped the bedroom carpet by one corner. In house after house the dangling carpets flap like welcoming flags above the scene of apparent hopelessness. Houses have collapsed inwards or upper storeys have fallen over into the next house, so that debris, clothing, furniture and household bits are mixed up.

A few shoves with a bulldozer and what's left of the village would return completely to the mountain.

But people under this sort of stress acquire a strange strength. So it is with these numbed but unbeaten survivors, tough peasants both men and women alike. Incredibly they are tackling this impossible heap with their bare hands. Little boys shout importantly when they turn up some battered but still recognisable bit of kitchenware.

They shout but they don't laugh. It is the first thing you notice when you enter the ruined village. After what they have seen and heard these usually irrepressible children look cowed, like children who have taken a beating.

A tented camp raised by the Army houses most of the survivors on the lower slopes of the village. But some families, with moving stubbornness, are camping beneath awnings spread in front of the rubble which was their home. They spend their days patiently piling the debris on one side and their salvaged belongings neatly on the other.

A woman with a water jug stopped, knelt before what had been a house and began swaying and keening. The house had been her home, they said, and her husband had died in it while she was out to fetch water.

The rubbish is turned over. Little intimate things come to light – a scrap of a dress, a chamber pot, a locket, a vest.

A shopkeeper, oblivious to all else, was digging out his safe.

A woman was on her knees before the one visible corner of her carpet, removing a 10ft pile of debris brick by brick. Her bedroom wall leaned drunkenly above her. Passing soldiers kept telling her about it. She dug on.

Some shopkeepers salvaged a few bits worth selling. At the shoe shop they were trying to match shoes.

In an archway, the front and rear walls of the shop having disappeared, one man was back in business with boiled sweets, nutmegs, chocolate biscuits and flypapers – and lentils just as soon as the boy had riddled them out of a heap of dust.

Another merchant had spread his remaining wares on hessian sacks on the pavement: goats' hair for spinning, nuts and dates and, incongruously, a blow-football set.

When it became too hot to work on the rubble the dust-caked men of the village gathered, as they always have done, around the cool ornamental pool at the crossroads. One ticked off a little boy for trampling on the remaining sweet peas. In the circumstances it seemed a remarkably civilised reproof.

As I was shaving at the municipal ornamental pool at dawn today I watched a small boy arrive at the crossroads with a barrow-load of melons. He spread an awning, set up his weighing machine, and within a minute had made a sale.

A broad smile transformed his serious little face. It wasn't exactly a laugh.

But for the moment, in this stricken land, it will do.

5 September 1968

CHAPTER ONE

The fjord has never been fjiner

TWO HUNDRED AND FIFTY MILES north of the Arctic Circle, 80 in the shade and, just along the beach, a bronzed, flaxen-haired beauty stark naked... I tell you, it's hell up here. For one thing, the blonde is about nine months old. And, for another, Mack's bar, the northernmost pub in the world, is in some danger of running out of beer. The Arctic Circle and I are basking in a freak heat-wave now in its third week. We're getting tourists from the south of *France.*

This is Tromso, 'capital' of northern Norway, a step from the North Cape, 70deg north latitude against London's 51. From here, Lapland is the Deep South, and even the reindeer are sweating.

Around midnight last night – well, not night exactly, because it's daylight around the clock – the temperature dropped to a chill 60 degrees, roughly the average daytime temperature in the north of England. At noon today, it topped 85. Even so, people were saying, just as they do in Blackpool or Bognor, 'You should have been here last week.' Last week it topped 90 degrees, the highest since they started keeping records 100 years ago. For a spell, at least, the weather has turned Norway upside down.

Back at Oslo Airport, 600 miles south, there wasn't much of a queue for the Costa del Sol. The planes to the Arctic were packed. From here I could fly to the North Pole in less time than it would take to get to Paris. Yet the ice-cream is melting in the shops.

Tromso, where an exciting day out usually doesn't extend much further than a pony trek or a visit to the whale factory, is a bit dazed by it all. So am I. My milk-white flesh, the envy of many a houri from Marrakech to the Gulf, got its first exposure to the sun this year within a nautical mile or two of where we sank the Tirpitz.

It caused quite a stir on the beach, not to mention a titter or two. Among the nut-brown beauties who had been soaking up the unpolluted sunshine for three weeks I stood out with all the charm of a 6ft slug. Whey-faced, I explained that I was from Britain, where a thermometer in Essex was struggling towards this year's record of 73 degrees. (They worked it back to 22 degrees Centigrade and gave me a pitying pat on the head.)

They're used to 'pleasant' summers in Tromso, pleasant enough to make the well-heeled take off for Italy or the Canaries. This year the palm trees (Heracleum sibiricum) are 8ft tall. Tromso Airport's single baggage handler wears shorts and plimsolls. There are parasols over garden tables, and farmers' wives and daughters are working in the fields in bikinis.

Due to the complexities of Norway's dairy system the nearest ice-cream factory is 200 miles away. It is now working 24 hours a day, and deliveries to Tromso have been doubled. But the 'deep freeze' cabinets in the ice-cream shops are not geared to this kind of weather, and the ice-cream is actually running in the freezers. To get a solid ice-cream, you have to nip in quickly behind the delivery van.

Mack's brewery – the most northerly in the world, and long may it prosper – usually turns out 350,000 bottles of beer and mineral water a day. Yesterday's production was 700,000 bottles, and even then they had to ration it around the bars. The brewery has its own pub on the premises, and the more ardent congregated there yesterday, confident that it would be the very last pub to run out of ale – though at 33 pence a glass, you'd wonder where they got the money.

The fjord has never been fjiner, and doctors are writing articles in the local newspaper about the effects of something called sunburn.

I could have fried an egg on the pavement in the central square, dominated by a statue of King Haakon, but for a certain uncertainty about Norway's stringent litter laws. So I stayed on the beach, among the stunningly beautiful housewives and their protective children, the businessmen who had sneaked away with swimming trunks in their briefcases, and watched the unseasonable sun melt permanent snow from high mountain gullies for the first time in living memory.

A brief Arctic Riviera is in full swing. The shops are being raided for the flimsy things people usually buy for the Mediterranean. Into

27

this sweltering scene there flew tonight a whole congress of marine insurance experts employed by a Norwegian firm. One of the 14 from England, perspiring in honest British broadcloth, moaned that he had been advised to bring a heavy dinner jacket. But there's hope yet. The latest met report says there's a depression moving north from the general direction of Britain. I hope so. I'm going home tomorrow.

7 July 1972

The cannibals were friendly

I WAS SHAVING waist deep in the Areguma, a pastry slice for a mirror, when this cannibal swam down the river bed and grabbed my ankles. Well, I mean, I'd searched London without success for a chrome mirror. The pastry slice, my wife's idea, was the ideal substitute. A girl in the chemist's had suggested a compact. I'm glad I said No. The cannibals, apart from a taste for homo sapiens, have another for homosexuality. Happily, the one who dug his nails into my ankles wanted only to play crocodiles.

Anyway, we were out-numbered – eight of us to 40 of them. They were the first cannibals any of us had seen. But then, we were the first pink British tourists they had seen. The mixed feelings were mutual.

This was our third day on the trail with them in one of the remoter parts of Papua New Guinea, and their initial shyness was giving way to smiles, and even bursts of hysterical laughter at our weird ways. Three days from London at a cost of £800 (£18 extra for the cannibal detour) Thomas Cook had landed its first tourists in the Stone Age.

The men frolicking in the river were the Biami, one of the most feared of tribes. They number only 3,300 but were 'tamed' as recently as 1969.

They ate their last barbecued bloke only a year ago. All they left of him fills a 2lb coffee jar in the office of the Assistant District Commissioner on the Nomad River. It was Exhibit A in a test case he prepared. As the law does not admit the existence of cannibalism, the charge was 'interfering with a corpse'. The judge threw it out.

As we surveyed our Biami porters the ADC, Robyn Barclay, a rangy, laconic Australian, said: 'You can bet on it that every one of them over 10 has eaten human flesh. And not for ritualistic reasons either. They do it for the meat.' Incidentally, the term 'long pig' is misleading. Apparently we taste much like cassowary, which is a sort of emu in Technicolor. And the cassowary is tough and gamey. Favourite cut is the ball of the thumb, nibbled daintily like a drumstick.

Fortunately, throughout the five days we spent in their villages, the Biami stuck to their usual diet of small sour cooking bananas baked in a wood fire, and sago. These are not the fine globules you encourage your kids to eat, but the dried, pink pith of the sago-palm, the consistency of gummy-dough, which they ram down a hollow bamboo and bake in the embers. It tastes like pith.

They guzzle 15lb of such carbohydrates a day, rarely taste protein except at a pig-killing feast, and yet they carried our 30lb packs up their one-in-four ridges at a fast walking pace and got their breath back running down the further slope. As we struck into the dank forest, the line of 40 porters set up a great ululation which shattered the cathedral quiet like a peal of bells. It is a chilling sound until you get used to it. It is a repetitive 'Wha-whoo,' with a yodel at the hyphen. There is a sort of counterpoint in it, and it has some of the form of an English round.

Off they went at a jog trot, their genitals in a string bag, thick skirts of brown straw flapping at their backsides. Stocky, pot-bellied men with six-inch bamboo tubes through their nose septums. The diameter varies with age – that of a cigarette for youths, half Coronas for their elders. A favourite police method of arresting a man so adorned is to hook the first and second fingers round the bamboo and pull downwards very hard.

Thomas Cook's pioneers into the Stone Age wore shirts, shorts, floppy jungle hats, thick woollen socks and rubber soled, calf-length jungle boots made in, of all places, Czechoslovakia. All quickly turned, and remained, the colour of sweat.

The first half-hour, downhill, was a delight. The temperature was high in the 90s and the humidity too. But there were exotic blossoms and a myriad butterflies, and the anticipation of being first into jungle visited only occasionally by government patrol officers. The villagers, timid at first, had never seen so many white people together before. But elation took a nose-dive when climbing the first ridge. I panted, I gasped. I told porters to pass on while I tried to pull in enough humid air to slow my hammering heart.

We forded a knee-deep river, drenching boots and socks, so that our feet took on a crinkled, parboiled look. I gratefully filled my hat with water and replaced it on my head, letting the shower soak shirt, shorts, cigarettes, paper handkerchiefs, everything. Then a 30ft sheer scramble up the further bank, grabbing at protruding roots. Then another 300ft ridge, and another, until we staggered into a knoll cleared of vegetation where a bamboo hut on stilts, erected for visiting patrol officers, was to be our first 'hotel'.

We flopped on to its dirty floor wheezing, waiting for our heartbeats to slow, astonished to find that we had been walking only two hours and covered less than four miles.

Now began the regular evening routine. Our guide, Rick Furlong, a 28-year-old unflappable Australian, and his cook-boy, David, erected a flat-roofed tent of mosquito netting where our food was prepared. Fried bully beef, spaghetti and peas, tinned peaches and lashings of tea from the billy was a typical evening meal. A flurry of instructions from English into pidgin English, the lingua franca, then into the local dialect, and the cannibals dug a latrine, screened by enormous palm fronds.

Another screen went up around a suspended canvas bucket which, at the turn of a nozzle, became a shower. We ate by the light of paraffin lamps. The cannibals squatted round their own fires, waiting for the sago-stuffed bamboo to burst with a bang. Occasionally they would drift out of the darkness to watch the mysteries of tins being opened, of sugar being stirred into tea. Their only drink was water, carried in six-foot bamboo sticks plugged with leaves. It's rather like trying to drink a yard of ale. Unless you have a steady hand, you get a face-full. (It was a source of wonder and, later, annoyance to discover that these people have never developed an alcoholic beverage).

Another ululation in the dusk announced the arrival of the women and children of the village back from their gardens in the jungle. Dressed only in skirts of bark, few were good looking, few were well made. The breasts of the elders hung like razor straps from a barber's chair. They lined up, each depositing at her feet a seemingly pathetic bunch of cooking bananas, taro, sago, or a few coconuts. Rick Furlong and an interpreter went down the line haggling for what was to be the porters' food for the following day. He paid in coin, bars of soap, a handful of much-sought-after salt. To feeding 40 porters – about £1 a day.

With nightfall, the birds of the jungle make a rapid, raucous tour of their territory, then fall quiet, leaving the night to twinkling fireflies and lumbering, bat-like flying foxes. For the first time in 40 years I was in bed at 7.30 pm.

David had the billy bubbling when we stirred at 5.30 am. The idea was to walk in the 'cool' of the morning, before the temperature hit 100 degrees. The sun belted only occasionally through the 100ft canopy of trees. If you looked up at it, if you so much as wiped your brow with your soaking hat, you risked a fall over a jutting root.

You walked, scrambled, clambered head down, your eyes flickering from the footsteps of the man in front to the sapling he was grabbing to steady himself down some slippery slope. Sometimes you gave in and slid down on your backside. At the bottom of a ridge, the porters ahead would run unerringly along a 40-foot tree trunk spanning a boggy stream, near-prehensile toes aiding perfect balance. After one undignified and extremely filthy fall from such a 'bridge' I took to straddling them and pulling myself along laboriously, bumpety-bump. The cannibals fell about. I did my best to smile.

But there were moments to savour. I lay in a shallow stream and an enormous blue emperor butterfly settled on my belly. Where we played crocodiles (we saw only one real one, and it ignored us) we saw for the first and only time in our lives hundreds upon hundreds of butterflies, an impossibly beautiful cloud of iridescence which stayed with us for hours, settling fearlessly on our hands and arms, in our hair.

We went into the brooding, stinking darkness of a Biami hut, 50 yards long and 50 feet wide, housing eight families of one clan. There were spears and bows and arrows ready for instant use behind a front 'door' made of stout logs which slot on top of each other to make an impassable barrier. The men sleep in one section, the women and children in another, with the prized pigs, an important source of wealth. Between is a raised 'sing-sing' platform from which an elder leads a sort of crude Gregorian chant. These cannibals have some surprisingly abstract poetry about their surroundings.

On racks there were string bags in which they suspend their dead for six days, stroking the exuded grease from the body to rub on their own skins. Definitely not the sort of chaps you'd like your sister to marry. But happy enough to laugh at strange antics like my fly trick. The flies, in infinite variety, came at dusk, and stuck. I had perhaps 100 on each bare leg. The cannibals stared open-mouthed when I cleared first one leg with a rub of insect repellent, then the other. Each evening, they asked for an encore.

CHAPTER ONE

On the last day's trek in cannibal country, on the last steep slope, I came near to uttering the ultimate cliché: 'Go on without me.' I had taken all the prescribed pills, yet I had paid four visits into the jungle, where it pays one to be very quick. I was rattling with salt tablets, yet I was bent over at a right angle, and the sweat from my brow filled a large leaf before I stopped gulping air. And I asked myself, not for the first time, what kind of a rich nut thinks this is a holiday?

4 December 1972

Will they be greeted with bullets or bougainvillea?

SAIGON, April 1975: Mulchrone described the approaching fall of the city to the Communists in daily reports right up to the end. Here are some of them:

WHEN I FIND A SPARE MINUTE I must track down the International Prawn Breeding Convention which is meeting somewhere in Saigon and ask what's new with scampi.

Saigon is not exactly the convention capital of the world these days, so the prawn boys strike a slightly crazy note of normality in an otherwise edgy city. Actually, it's not as daft as it sounds. With their lumber and rubber plantations overrun by the Communists, prawns are now South Vietnam's biggest export. They are closely followed by duck feathers.

There is an Australian in my hotel who made a million shipping them to pillows around the world.

At the airport they are still hard at work on a new terminal building designed, after the Paris peace talks, to cope with a tourist boom. Today, the travellers go one way – out. Out to anywhere. All flights out of the country are booked solid for a week ahead.

A capital in panic then? On the surface there's not much sign of it, though nerves are taut as bowstrings. Even after the bombing attack on Thieu's palace the President's five-hour curfew disrupted life for only a short while. For once the steel anti-riot screens were pulled down over the shopfronts and the usually jammed streets became suddenly deserted. But when the curfew was lifted, what is accepted as normality here again took over.

If there is panic it is disguised. Much depends on how you read the signs. The people queuing at the banks are closing their accounts and taking away the piles of weakened currency in carrier bags. They are the ones who reckon the Communists will attack Saigon in weeks, perhaps days. There is only one question in this city – when?

In a handsome, tree-lined street, a legacy of French colonialism, I paused at a crossroad to admire a giant bougainvillea. It took a second look to see that it half hid a new pillbox. The machine-gun muzzle poked between the blossoms. And there you have it. When the Communists come, will they be greeted with bullets, or showered with bougainvillea? Will the South Vietnamese, who have taken so much for so long, fight again, or will they stick jasmine blossoms into Communist gun barrels?

The man in the street – in this case the sales manager of a bus company – says: 'Nobody knows. Nobody. It is the uncertainty that gets you down. There is a terrible atmosphere of suspicion everywhere. Nobody knows who is a secret Communist.' Yet Saigon, raucous with the sound of what must be scores of thousands of motor scooters, gets on with its work and its shopping until the 9 pm curfew leaves the streets, barricaded with barbed wire, until 6 am to the soldiers. In the festering slums behind the facade of colonial villas, the poor squat over bowls of noodle soup cooked at pavement stalls. Old women beg with empty tin cans, following 'round-eyes' – any Westerner – until their old legs give out.

The Americans have long gone, now, and the street markets have run out of stolen 'K' rations. But they still bulge with 'liberated' American equipment – boots, uniforms, radios, cameras.

A sign of the times, maybe, but the British Club, which is above a brothel in the main street of the city, has relaxed its rule about having to wear a tie.

At aperitif time, prostitutes stroll past the city's most famous rendezvous, the open terrace of the Continental Palace Hotel, all wickerwork chairs and ceiling fans. But light conversation is difficult when the loudspeakers erected in the square blast out the patriotic urgings of President Thieu. Then martial music and choruses deafen you. One of the recorded bands, which includes a large flute section, has a tune reminiscent of Orange Order marching songs on July 12.

Pretty little girls hawk necklaces of jasmine blossom. If you buy they say, 'You Number One.' If you don't, they call after you 'Cheap Charlie.' That's probably how they'll remember us 'round-eyes' after we have hurried to the airport for the last time.

9 April 1975

The Union Jack is lowered and put away

AT FIVE MINUTES past four local time here the Union Jack was lowered from its mast, and the British Embassy in Saigon temporarily ceased to exist. 'This is an evacuation for the safety of lives,' said Ambassador John Bushell, before he left the Embassy in his Jaguar. Behind him he left a Vietnamese staff of 36, who have been paid in advance, and who are expected to maintain the building until the diplomats return.

The 70 who were going gathered in the Embassy Club with its swimming pool still filled, its bar open to the last. On the walls hung prints of that Tudor building in Holborn and a coaching inn in Southwark. They climbed into their Land Rovers, leaving a library of paperbacks ranging from John Creasey thrillers to *The Tale of Timmy Tiptoes* by Beatrix Potter.

They didn't take the Union Flag with them. They left it at the Embassy with orders that it should be washed and pressed for next time. If, that is, there is one.

They were the lucky ones. For every one of them there were hundreds more trying to flee this increasingly desperate situation. Saigon is now for the taking. Many of the Britons have gone. The Americans are going. Of the 'round eyes' only the French remain.

They stay behind in a city where the rumour factories are working overtime. Clutching at straws yesterday people told each other there had been a coup d'état in Hanoi, and that four of the Communist divisions threatening Saigon were being pulled back to deal with it. What was distressingly true was that Communist forces were tightening their squeeze on the capital – now a city of three and a half million people, many of them refugees who have stopped running.

The beggars are becoming more desperate. Even those on crutches will follow you painfully for 100 yards. If you are seen to give what amounts to a few pence, you are immediately surrounded by old women pointing to their mouths, their bellies. If they fail, they send toddlers running after you, crying piteously for money for food. Some are professional beggars. But not all. And how can you decide between one and the other as you try to hurry on your business, which can have little effect on their fate?

I never thought I'd have a sense of guilt from having a return ticket to London in my pocket, but it happens daily now.

But these are tiny signs of fear compared with the flood of refugees who still have a little money and are trying to buy their way out of the country. They have given up any hope of getting an exit visa and flying out of Saigon airport, which will be within range of Communist anti-aircraft guns any hour now.

Of course the really rich had already gone to join their numbered accounts in Switzerland and Hong Kong – but the desperation of the situation has hit home to the mere 'comfortably off' only in the last few days.

On the streets of the city the *Saigon Post* was appearing with ads like this one which summed up an ocean of despair. It read: Fairly pretty high-school girl, 18, holder of the baccalaureate degree, piano player, of well-to-do family, seeks adoption by, or marriage with foreigner (of American, French, British, German or other nationality) who would take her abroad legally to enable her to continue her college studies outside Vietnam at her own expense.

First you admire the honesty that went into the words 'fairly pretty'. Then you feel sad for the family prepared to go to such lengths to save their daughter. Because, there is little doubt, they have left it too late.

Many of them have the added handicap of having been connected in some way with the Americans – yet not well enough to secure places on their airlift out. So they are fleeing in anything that will sail down the Saigon River to the port of Vung Tau, where, for money, and especially for American dollars, coasters of 300 tons are prepared to make for Bangkok or Singapore.

But dollars are increasingly hard to come by. They are a pretty reliable barometer of panic here. The official rate of exchange is 740 piastres to the American dollar. When the Communists began rolling down the coast, the black market rose to 2,000 to the dollar. Two days ago, the street traders were offering 3,000 to the dollar. Last night the rate was 4,500. That's how scared they are in Saigon.

25 April 1975

Escape from the doomed city

JINKING AND WEAVING at treetop height, we flew out of besieged Saigon yesterday, amid the screaming of the babies, the screaming of our nerves.

Behind and below our helicopter desperate Vietnamese fought with American Marines in an attempt to get on the last rescue flights – either from Saigon's airport or from the rooftops at the US Embassy compound. At times, the Marines and armed civilians had to use gun butts to smash the hands of the Vietnamese trying to climb over the 10ft Embassy wall. But the mass was so great that scores got over.

An hour after taking off, I was sipping a Coke and watching a cowboy movie on television in a mess hall in the ship, which is the 'Brains' of one of the most incredible evacuations in history.

For the lucky ones, the evacuation of Saigon was as sudden and as stunning as that. One minute you were flinching at the distinctive crack of Communist rockets and the next secure in the greatest armada since the second world war, being fed beef stew and tinned peaches by a carefree, laughing, Negro cook.

Thanks to the guts, and some blood, of the US Marines and Navy flyers, they did what many thought impossible without great loss of life. In about 18 hours 70 helicopters shuttled into and out of Saigon to pluck 6,500 people from death, or the fear of it, and deposited them safely on the ships of the Seventh Fleet. The 6,500 is misleadingly low because as we soared to the safety of the South China Sea over the port of Vung Tau the water was suddenly alive with ships.

Another kind of Dunkirk operation was going on as hundreds of small craft crammed with refugees raced for freighters chartered by the Americans.

The Vietnamese, some babes in arms, some old and frail, stared at an historic sight. They smiled, then cowered back on the helicopter floor as the machine gunner sitting at the open rear door threw out an exploding flare to lure away Sam heat-seeking missiles.

Even before dawn on Tuesday, it was obvious the Communists had Tan Son Nhut airport under such heavy rocket attack that an evacuation by fixed wing aircraft was out of the question.

At sun-up, with the city under a 24-hour curfew, it was obvious that the old, gay Saigon had gone for ever. This was a sullen, terrified city, peering through its shutters at groups of foreigners and Vietnamese dependants making their way to secure, American-owned buildings which were to be the pickup points for buses to the airport. And there was envy and hate in some of the stares, and tears in some of the eyes.

30 April 1975

FOOD AND DRINK

The five happiest words I've written

I DO BELIEVE I am about to write what may be the most beautiful sentence in the English language. And not merely beautiful, but also unique. The five words are ordinary enough in themselves. But they have never come together in this order before because the magic moment they capture has never happened before.

But first I'll have to take you to Jimmy McGuinness' pub in Monaghan. You'd never find it by yourself. It has no sign. It never had. For as long as anybody can remember the pub has preserved its discreet anonymity – just another house in a terrace in Mill Street.

But talk about character. For a start, it looked as if it hadn't been dusted since Queen Elizabeth's coronation. The first Elizabeth, that is. Half its space was taken up by six snugs, those dark little stalls which the Irish use for plotting, or for discussing birth control, or for pretending that they don't frequent pubs.

Behind the bar old Jimmy reigned alone. He pretty well had to because, behind the bar, there wasn't room for more than one pair of feet. The rest was taken up by bottles, emptied by dead generations, and by a heap of correspondence, some of it 40 years old, which had assumed the shape and proportions of a miniature landslide. All that was left for the customers, between snugs and bar, was a narrow, uncomfortable, stone-flagged passageway.

Any student of pubs will recognise at once that this combination of discomforts was bound to attract intelligent drinkers on the run from pressurised beers, plastic bar-tops, chrome fittings and TV. Add to this the fact that Jimmy was a notable stirrer of political argument, a tight-lipped confidant, a trusty friend, and an idiosyncratic barman, and you will see that this was a pub well above the ruck. The professional and business leaders of the town thought so, anyway. Into that narrow passage were crowded doctors and lawyers and civil servants and butchers – all drawn by the highly individualistic appeal of what a man likes to call 'his' pub.

Then the blow fell. Jimmy announced that he was going to retire. The death of a loved one apart, there are few crises in a man's life comparable to the wretchedness of being faced with a new landlord. The old familiarity and ease, built up carefully over the years, dies before your eyes. The pub reverts to being a building again. The sense of loss is real and profound. No matter how pleasant, skilful and even ingratiating he may be, the new landlord holds such terrors that he can split an old-established pub clientele asunder, fragmenting their carefully constructed camaraderie, and forcing on them the dreadful necessity of working their way into other pubs.

In a pub like Jimmy's the fear went especially deep. There was even some wild talk, quickly stifled, about giving up drinking. And then came the glorious idea, so simple and so flawless that they are laughing still in wonder at it. With one perfect stroke they banished the nightmare and made a drinking man's dream come true.

You have been very patient. Here comes the sentence nobody has ever written before:

The customers bought the pub.

They should have set the words to a fanfare. They should put it on a flag or strike a gold medallion. They slapped each other on the back, and they bought the boozer.

They took a count of the firm regulars. And 26 of them chipped in and bought it. Twenty-six of the happiest landlords in the world. When they're all in, the pub's full. And when the till tinkles, 26 pairs of eyes flicker with delight. They have a barman who works for all 26 of them. The service is perfect. They have got a 21-year lease for a mere £2,100. Some bought a share for as little as £25. Some have £50 in it, some £100. The most anybody has invested is £150.

The world's most democratic pub has been open a week and it's doing great business. Most of it from its landlords.

4 November 1967

CHAPTER TWO

Backwards through the à la carte

I LUNCHED BACKWARDS YESTERDAY. 'Good morning sir,' said the waiter. 'Goodbye,' I replied, and for an aperitif ordered coffee and brandy. He reacted with an aplomb which, if you could bottle the stuff, would be worth a guinea a sniff. 'Certainly, sir,' he said, and passed on the order to an equally inscrutable *commis*.

'Then,' I said with increasing firmness, I'll have La Tranche d'Ananas au Kirsch, *followed* by roast beef and Yorkshire pudding. And to follow – soup. A little chilled Vichyssoise.'

He didn't bat an eyelid. He reacted to my choice with such pleasure (as a waiter should) that I thought he was going to smack his lips. Taking firm control of a mounting hysteria I went on: 'And last of all I'll have a glass of dry sherry.'

The iron-nerved servant inscribed a last hieroglyphic on his pad and, without a trace of irony, asked: 'Would you like some olives and nuts with the sherry, sir?'

In a vain effort to regain control of the situation I told him (as if he wasn't already aware) that my purpose was to lunch backwards. 'Of course, sir,' he said. 'Would you prefer the bill *now?*' (There must be *something* that would shake the waiters at the Savoy Grill. I have a private yearning to go there one day and order braised Macedonian mountain stoat. Except, they'd only say, 'Yes, sir. Male or female?').

I was too humbled to reveal that I was eating backwards in the cause of science. A certain Dr Howard H Raper, writing in the American magazine *Dental Survey,* says eating backwards is OK. If you eat the sweet first, he says, later courses scour away the sugar which promotes tooth decay. And weight-conscious adults, says the good dentist, find that starting with dessert kills the appetite.

It didn't, I may as well say, kill mine. (Except that anybody who can finish his soup *after* roast beef is a better man than I).

But I must say the experiment induced some fairly fanciful impressions on the side. The first was that the kirsch you get on pineapple kills the taste of brandy stone dead. And the second, that horseradish sauce acts like paint-stripper on kirsch. The soup, as I have said, made little impression.

It was with some difficulty that the waiter dissuaded me from mounting my table and addressing my fellow slaves, all meekly eating their way through the Savoy menu in the hallowed, top-to-bottom fashion. 'You're nothing compared with some people, sir,' he said.

'*Some* people,' said the waiter, 'start with the sweet trolley. And I've seen some start with scrambled eggs and coffee, go through the menu and finish with smoked salmon.' And he squared his shoulders and thrust his thumbs into line with the braid on his trousers. A very brave man, I thought.

15 June 1962

Where fish and chips first met

THE NEW PLACE OF PILGRIMAGE is opposite the bus stop, next to the Stamford Arms, Mossley, Lancs. About every half-hour it gives off a fierce crackle. Mostly, though, it just sits there, steaming gently. You get the best view from across the market place, with your back to the Methodist church notice-board which says:

> *Every time I pass a church,*
> *I pay a little visit:*
> *So when at last I'm carried in*
> *The Lord won't say:*
> *'Who is it?'*

The lights in the little shop are usually the last in the town to go out. That's the way it is with fish and chip shops.

This shop, according to recent research, may be the oldest in the country. What is more exciting to us addicts is that this may prove to be the spot where fish and chips first came together in that magical union in which the

41

succulent sum is greater than the parts. If so, the hagiography of those inspired mystics who first mated such improbables as roast beef and Yorkshire, apple pie and cheese, kippers and marmalade, will be headed by one John Lees, father of fish and chips.

For it really is an extraordinary, and extraordinarily *emotional* dish. I have seen sahibs salivate at the mention of them. I have heard bishops, colonial governors, captains of industry talk of a fish and four penn'orth with a catch in the voice. I do it myself. When I was a lad the weavers would send a couple of weft lads for an order of '85 times'. They carried them back to the mill, Indian file, in a sack slung between their shoulders. The sack steamed in the face of the lad behind. And it was a treat just to walk behind *him.*

I have never sought to have the alchemy of smell and taste and nostalgia explained. Any more than I would ever want to know how the conjurer does it. The magic itself is sufficient. But the trade has decided, somewhat arbitrarily, that this year is the centenary of the birth of fish and chips. And those pesky psychiatrists have got in on the act. They have rationalised the peculiar appeal of the dish into a yearning for the carefree days of youth when a packet of fish and chips put the seal on a good night out. But psychiatrists live in London, where the disturbed minds are. And there *are* no good fish and chips in London, so who are they to talk?

The best fish and chips are to be found in the heavy woollen district of the West Riding. It is only there, and in a few isolated pockets scattered about the country, that they still create the original, deep golden brown fish and chips which can be obtained only by using the best beef dripping. Even Lancashire's gone to hell. They used to use lard, which was passable. Now it's vegetable oil. What London uses I shudder to think.

London? Phooey. Up here, at least, they stick to haddock and skate and cod. London gives you dubious dogfish, under the tarted-up name of rock salmon. They neither skin nor fillet the fish. We've always known they were a mucky lot. It beats me that Harold Wilson sticks the place. Me, too, for that matter.

The shop in Mossley is kept by a one-armed Irishman and his Welsh wife, which should surprise nobody, for it is a trade which breeds characters. The centenary has attracted officials from the White Fish Authority, television cameras even. An unlikely claim to similar antiquity from an Eastbourne fish and chip establishment has already been repulsed with a fine show of civic indignation. It looks as though the wall plaque offered by the National Federation of Fish Fryers to 'the oldest fish and chip business in the world' will find its home here.

The records of this business go back 102 years. When King Edward VII was crowned somebody photographed the decorated shop front and, with it, the legend 'Lees' Chip Potato Restaurant. Oldest Estd. in the World.' Chips, yes. But when did the fish join? The Federation itself, after some remarkably intensive research, doesn't know which joined which, or when, or where.

The French gave us chips. *Oliver Twist* (1850) has a mention of a 'fried fish warehouse.' A *Times* reporter of the 1850s, Henry Mayhew, described people frying fish in their own homes to hawk, cold, in the streets. It was eaten with hunks of bread.

Still alive, at 72, is Mr Joe Lees, grandson of the founder, who followed his own father in the business. And he, at least, is sure about it. 'My grandfather John definitely sold fish *and* chips.' If he did, he was quite possibly the first to do so. I'll bet he turned to his wife one day and said: 'Annie. Ah'm fed up wi' saveloys and black puddins. How do you think chips and *fish* would go?'

And I'll bet she turned to him, hair all lank in the steam from the chip pan, and said: 'Fish *and* chips? Nay, John, lad, who ivver heard of fish and chips?' At least I hope she said that. I mean, if we're going to have a legend we've got to start somewhere.

13 November 1965

It must be hell to know you're an oyster

SOME OF THE WORLD'S NICEST KILLERS gathered here today, each with a small armoury of wickedly curved knives. As they compared blades and wrist actions, an onlooker was heard to thank heaven that there was still room for a little insanity in the world.

CHAPTER TWO

Galway's annual oyster festival, long one of the happiest riots in the Western world, is about to stage history's first international oyster opening contest. And the competitors have brought their own hardware.

As an idea it is superbly daft, brilliantly pointless. Everybody knows, or should, that the painless way to open oysters is to place them on a hot oven plate. They gape open in sheer fright. But no. Opening oysters is a part of the mystique which has always attached itself to the weird bivalve. People use pincers, hammers and even door jambs before risking a knife and the usual stab wound in the palm of the left hand.

To open oysters against a stopwatch must be one of the last areas of competition left open to man. And Galway Bay, where millions of the cold-blooded invertebrates live, is a superb setting for the world's first Oyster Olympics.

Part of the Irish genius for fun lies in the way grown men address themselves seriously to inconsequentialities. And the twinkle in Galway's eye was only just kept in check today when poker-faced, leading citizens met the contestants to draw up the rules. Historically, this may prove as important as the day the Marquis of Queensberry said no hitting below the belt, or the first meeting of the Royal and Ancient.

Sensing the importance of the contest Air France flew the competitors in from England, France, Germany, the US and Canada. From a fish restaurant in Brighton, to represent Great Britain, comes Frederick Lassetter, 55 years old, with rimless spectacles, looking like a comfortably off businessman. He reckons he must have opened a couple of million oysters in a lifetime in fish restaurants.

Germany's entrant is 23-year-old Werner Pippig, who opens oysters at Hamburg's famous Schoemans Austernkeller. After a knock-out competition in Montreal, Canada sent Jean Raynaud, 25-year-old chef from McGill University. The French competitor, and a bit of a dark horse, is Albert Duret, 38, a dumpy little man with a lugubrious moustache, who works in a fish market in Lyons. The American contestant discovered at the last minute that he had no birth certificate and, therefore, couldn't travel. The Western sky is being scanned for his last minute replacement.

The Irish champion will be decided by competition at a ball in the early hours of tomorrow.

The Irish, who will bet on anything capable of movement, are vaguely disturbed by this entirely new sport. 'There's no *form,* d'ye see,' said an anguished punter who was hanging around in the hope of opening a book.

Such form as there is rests in the performance of a little Frenchman to whom everyone shows deference. Monsieur Williams Bley, sporting a

Breton fisherman's casquette and a cigar, is the acknowledged world champion – having publicly opened 100 oysters in three minutes 37 seconds. He will head the panel of judges. By comparison, professional oyster-openers in the West End of London reckon they are doing well if they manage to open eight a minute.

In a babel of tongues, the rules were decided. Each contestant will open 50 oysters against a stop-watch. A mutilated oyster will incur a one-second penalty.

The poor oyster. A creature rhapsodic or revolting according to your taste; it has two hearts, a wheel in its stomach, changes sex every year and is falsely credited with aphrodisiac properties.

Whelk tingles bore into them; starfish suck them dry with a sort of vacuum cleaner. Oyster-catchers drop them from a great height to crack their shells. And now they are in the Olympics. Come to think of it, it must be hell to wake up of a morning and know that you're an oyster.

21 September 1968

The fearless tin-opener strikes again

WIELDING MY FEARLESS PEN like a tin-opener, I now return to the worrying subject of pineapple chunks. I said the other day, in a moment of moving honesty, I prefer pineapple chunks to the fresh fruit. The trouble is, as I said, that though pineapple *chunks* are part of our birthright, the country is being swamped by an insidious flood of pineapple *bits*.

Carried away, I confessed to a preference for many tinned foods – tinned salmon supreme among them. And pears. And peaches. And artichoke hearts. Oh, and green figs, new potatoes, crab and apricots. The response from readers has been such that I do believe I have come across a sort of canned underground – possibly millions of people who have been waiting for a fearless tin-opener like myself before daring to profess that they actually prefer tinned to fresh.

And nothing sluttish about it. Take playwright John Osborne, not exactly a slouch when it comes to pricking our little snobberies. He wrote 'What a fabulous hymn to tins! And the Divine Chunks. And asparagus tips. And, of course, salmon. For some years I was obliged to open it like a wartime resistance worker listening to the BBC.'

Once again, Mr Osborne puts his finger right on the spot. It has taken too much out of us, all these years, to open tins *furtively*. Thank heaven it's all out in the open now. Osborne, who needs no lessons in courage from me, goes further.

'I feel the same about mayonnaise,' he says. 'Can't stand the *real* stuff made with eggs and *real* lemon.' (God, but you have to admire that man.) 'Have no attachment to frozen food at all – but tins, glorious tins. I'm opening one for lunch with a bottle of Pouilly Fumé.'

But hold hard, Osborne. Mr Holman of West Byfleet, Surrey – a chunk man, and therefore one of us – cautions against the innocent delight of crunching (tinned) salmon bones.

'Don't you know,' he asks (and he is a BSc – and, to boot, a FBPsS) 'that the true salmon bones are osseous (calcified) and therefore unchewable, and that the bones inserted in salmon tins are those of the dogfish, one of the Elasmobranchs, which are cartilaginous, and therefore chewable?' Well no, I didn't. And still don't. Kindly leave the stage, Mr Holman.

I have had scores of letters telling me that you still get chunks in this village store or that. And I am happy for you all. A woman doctor in my part of Surrey has put me on to a chunk shop. Like many others, she describes the product perfectly – 'succulent, that is not woody, tasty and inexpensive.'

And an Acton firm threatens to send me a canned fish-cake, orange dessert, stuffed baked apple, and spaghetti with mini-burgers. And why not?

Why not tinned Champagne – very handy for the fridge? Or tinned fish and chips, made north of the Wash and sold to Southerners who scarcely know what the real thing tastes like? And if you come up with any ideas about how to tin chip butties, just drop me a line...

6 August 1968

Champagne – it's never been in such a tizzy

BOUZY. AND never a French village better named, unless you count the place down the road called Dizy. Both stand in a countryside stunned by a phenomenon of nature. For no earthly reason, the champagne harvest has doubled itself.

It is an event as remarkable – though about ten times as expensive – as the hop fields of Kent deciding, without human agency, to double the production of British beer.

If nature had behaved naturally, the grape harvest in the 50,000 exclusive acres allowed to call themselves champagne would have been over last Friday. As things are the harvest won't be over for another seven days. There has never been such a harvest in recorded history. And there is absolutely no explanation for it. The earth, the weather decided it. On these grey hills the grapes are growing in tight clusters as firm as a boxing glove, and at very near double their best rate.

In its biggest years the Champagne district has never produced much more than 90 million bottles. Conservative estimates for this harvest predict 170 million bottles.

From Bouzy to Dizy the Champagne has never been in such a tizzy. Little men with a single hectare (2.4 acres) of vines who would normally net £2,750 will get double that for their crop. Outside the Maison de la Champagne in Epernay I met Christian Pol Roger, 29, dressed in immaculate English tweeds, and declaring with some passion: 'I would sell my tie to invest in wine this year.'

And M. Pol Roger is a man of discrimination when it comes to ties.

When the blind monk Dom Perignon 'invented' champagne, he uttered one of the most memorable sayings about drink since St Paul's 'a little wine for thy stomach's sake.' He is supposed to have called out to his brothers: 'Come quickly – I am drinking stars.'

CHAPTER TWO

It is that sort of wine. As Mme Lily Bollinger says: 'I drink it when I'm happy and when I'm sad. Sometimes I drink it when I am alone. When I have company I consider it obligatory. I trifle with it if I am not hungry and drink it when I am. Otherwise I never touch it – unless I am thirsty.'

All very fine. But what took me to Champagne in this extraordinary year was the fact, which shook the champagne houses no end, that last year the British started to go off champagne.

Since Edward VII we have been, and we remain, their biggest export market.

But where we drank 6,900,000 bottles in 1968, the figure plummeted to 5,500,000 bottles in 1969.

Curiously, exports to Britain have been recovering this year, and there is at least one champagne expert who claims it could be due to our political climate.

'It is an historical fact that the British drink champagne when they are feeling confident,' says the 39-year-old Viscomte Bernard de la Giraudiere. The handsome viscomte sells champagne for the venerable house of Laurent Perrier.

In 1969's dull political climate, cheaper sparkling wines made inroads into champagne sales.

'If the political theory is true,' he says, 'then 1969 was a year of no confidence at all. Certainly a lot of champagne was sold in Britain as a result of the 1970 election, and figures generally are recovering. It may have to do with the higher price of spirits, but more and more people in Britain are drinking champagne as an aperitif.'

We talked in dark, dank cellars, among six million bottles patiently 'throwing' their sediment for three years before seeing the light. Even such massive cellars cannot cope with the harvest now being gathered above. Every spare wine vat in France has been brought in, and barges equipped to transport wine have been moored in the Marne canal to store the excess first pressings provided by the happy explosion of nature.

'This is a harvest like we have never seen before,' said Bernard de la Giraudiere. 'We shall have some wonderful wine for Britain in about four years' time. Provided,' he added dryly, 'that the climate over there is right.' I said I thought it would be. So he cracked a bottle and we drank to that.

13 October 1970

Bangers are as personal as religion

I MADE A SAUSAGE YESTERDAY. It was 24ft long and stuffed with pork and port, marjoram and mace. My youngest bore it over his shoulder like a hawser, and his end was half-way up the hall before mine ran out of the ambrosial extrusion in the kitchen. Everybody to his own idea of the good life. This happens to be mine.

The dimly remembered quality, the childhood goodness of so much of our food is being devalued *all* the time. The generations sit like rabbits before stoats while 'they' standardise and plasticise our bread, our kippers, our peas, our palates.

There's little one can do about the Chancellor. But I have a mincer, two hands, and a bit of imagination left.

And I have decided to halt the devaluation of taste in at least one important sector – that of bangers.

Bangers to the British are damn near as personal as religion – and to many a deal more alive as an issue.

As a single article of faith keeps the theologian busy, so has the sausage taxed, tried or titillated the utterances of judges, gourmets and the broader comedians. No other single offering to British tastebuds has been so despised, condemned, researched, reported on, recommended, or regulated.

Such passions have been aroused that we are to try to control the sausage with an Act, as if it were a pleasure like sex or drink, and had to be kept in check.

It will change the average banger hardly at all. And the average banger, in run-down Britain, has become a flaccid finger of stodge, a bland blend of legal minima, a uniform envelope which looks like wallpaper fixative and sometimes tastes the same when cooked.

My sausage, by contrast, is an ungainly beast, an ugly, awkward, gawky thing with an occasional nipped-in waist where my hand contracted when the phone rang. It is a rough and rugged fellow, a second-row forward of a sausage. Its muscles of pork and veal strain against the taut skin, showing themselves speckled with herbs.

Mine sometimes explode with sheer joy, which means I can guarantee crispy, burnt bits at the end – and sometimes in the middle. Your standard sausage won't do that, because basically it is impotent.

Mine, on the other hand, is the kind you wouldn't want your sister to marry.

The shop sausage looks as if it is waiting for a blood transfusion. Mine could give it one.

You need a mincing machine, of course, a coarse-screen mincer, the plastic tube which is the sausage filler, and a butcher who will sell you the skin. It costs about 2d. a yard, though I tried eight butchers before I got it ('Nobody *makes* sausages, sir').

For a family-size batch, buy 1lb. of lean pork, ½lb. of fat pork, ½lb. of lean veal and mince it coarsely. Mix together ½lb. of breadcrumbs, the grated rind of half a lemon, grated sage (say 12 leaves), one tsp. black pepper, two tsp. salt, ½tsp. marjoram, ½tsp. seasoning, ½tsp. mace, and half a glass of port. Mix all this with the meat and pass all through the mincer, pulling the skin off the sausage filler at an even rate. (You'll get the instructions with it.)

The following reactions occur in sequence: panic when the sausage starts over-flowing the table; bliss when you taste a rich morsel which is 80% meat; more bliss when you cost them at 5s. a lb. and a sublime smugness when you realise that you have struck your first blow against the great plastic food menace.

Revolt has to start somewhere, and the British eat 600,000 miles of sausages a year. I can think of worse banners than the banger.

9 December 1967

Why can't they leave our pubs alone?

THEY'VE JUST DESTROYED one of my locals. They didn't actually pull the pub down. They spent £45,000 'improving it'. And I am not alone in wishing they hadn't. I don't want an 'improved' pub.

The one they've 'improved' is much cleaner than the old one. It has more bars, each with a fancy name, each more cosy than the next, polished pine and black plastic banquettes inviting custom that, predictably, has disappeared.

What this country needs is a Lament for the Pub. The new Poet Laureate (who, I happen to know, has a proper reverence for malt whisky) should make it his first priority.

When she has a spare moment, the monarch should command her personal poet to cast his bleak eye on the extruded foam wattle ceilings and the polystyrene oak beams which look down on the Briton supping his over-carbonated beer.

Betjeman on the British pub would be bound to gain the brewer's ear. It's obvious that you and I cannot, otherwise they wouldn't tart up perfectly pleasant pubs and turn them into stage sets. If you haven't got a Smugglers' Den or a Mississippi Showboat bar in your local Red Lion, don't feel smug about it. It's only a matter of time.

Lord Mancroft, president of the London Tourist Board and not a man who minces words, had a go at the brewers at their own exhibition at Crystal Palace the other day.

CHAPTER TWO

As he told me: 'More and more, when you are looking for a glass of beer, you find yourself in a replica of the cockpit of Nelson's Victory or in something not far removed from a Dior boutique. All I want is a pub that looks like a pub. It should be scrupulously clean, have good loos, and preferably serve draught bitter.'

Add a tap room with a floor of stone flags, a roaring fire, a dartboard, and settles polished by generations of boozers' backsides, and I would happily try to drink Lord Mancroft under the table. But, even should he accept such an unlikely challenge, we'd have to hurry before they changed the old place into The Pickwick Bar, or the Jacobean Snug with, naturally, an extra penny on the pint.

It is difficult to pin down the spoilers, and equally difficult to argue with people who want to improve pubs without upsetting the delicate balance of a unique institution.

Mr Robert Neame is chairman of one of the largest remaining independent breweries, with 215 pubs in Kent and Surrey, many of them in need of some kind of modernisation.

'It is terribly important that the character of a pub should not be ruined,' he says, 'too much money is being spent on re-vamping pubs. I really believe it is the duty of independent brewers to maintain some sanity in the matter of a pub being a pub, part of the British way of life, which must not be destroyed by chrome and plushiness.'

His feelings are echoed by Michael Jacks who, at 37, is responsible for the decor of 3,000 Ind Coope pubs. I have seen, and have admired, his work. His philosophy about the atmosphere of drinking is unexceptionable.

'I like a pub with a good drinking atmosphere,' he says. 'Some ghastly things have been perpetuated to try to achieve this. Recently we have had Victoriana and Edwardiana rammed down our throats. Pubs today are too often fake. They con the customer until the novelty wears off. Then he goes back to his old drinking atmosphere, which is why people drive miles out into the countryside to get the genuine pleasure of drinking.'

I happen to like my grandfather's pub, where the cast iron tables are topped with wafer-thin copper and the beer is cooled in a cellar cut out of the local stone.

I don't want to leave my own grandchildren a heritage of plastic Pickwick Bars, where the beer can be made to foam at will, and the manager dreams of closing time.

I think it's not too much to ask.

28 October 1972

MULCHRONE'S BRITAIN

Cold in his coffin he was no less an inspiration

TWO RIVERS RUN SILENTLY through London tonight, and one is made of people. Dark and quiet as the night-time Thames itself, it flows through Westminster Hall, eddying about the foot of the rock called Churchill. And for all the tears and the stiff, awkward movements of Englishmen ashamed to give in to mourning, the first day of the lying-in-state of Sir Winston Churchill is ending on a note well removed from grief.

If you could distil the emotion that has flowed through England's most venerable hall today into a sound the heart would recognise, it would never fit the plaintive oboe. You would have to play it bravely, distantly, on a bugle made for war.

People grieving give up something of themselves. The people who came back to Churchill today seemed, on the contrary, to be drawing some intangible strength from *him*. Cold in his coffin, he was no less an inspiration. It showed itself in many ways as the true tapestry of England – not the braided, glinting highlights of ceremonial, but the rough and ready weave of the people – went by.

There was no form, scarcely any precedent, so people did the best they knew, out of rich diversity of background and breeding. Tall, soldierly men came to the sort of attention which must have hurt their old backs and, without breaking the smooth pace of those pressing behind, bowed their heads in a clipped military way. There were some, even, who managed to fall on both knees as they passed the catafalque and immediately rise without ostensibly embarrassing those behind.

Some blessed themselves with the Sign of the Cross. Some shook their heads as though impatient with death for taking him away. Some even seemed to walk by without looking up at the coffin. But all, without exception, looked back. Before they left the north door of the hall, some instinct of history made them pause, turn, and take a last look at the scene.

The incredibly patient queue grew and shrank with the passing hours. But for most of the day it stretched two or three deep, from the St Stephen's entrance to the House of Commons, along Millbank, across Lambeth Bridge, and turned back on itself along the South Bank of the Thames almost to St Thomas's Hospital, forming three sides of an oblong.

They went into the Palace of Westminster by the route many a commoner has gone to see the MP who lay there tonight. But instead of going straight ahead to the central lobby, they turned left and came in a slow cascade down the steps into Westminster Hall. The chief illumination came from soft lights directed on to the bronze forest of Sussex oak which is the glorious hammerbeam roof of the Hall.

Below, all was as grey and chill as the atmosphere which pervaded the Hall, save for the catafalque area, lit by six saffron-coloured candles. Day-long, the three Services took part in the death watch over their old chief. The Navy, the Guards, the strangely young successors of The Few who fought the Battle of Britain, succeeded each other at the four corners of the catafalque. For a brief time this morning there happened one of those splendid bursts of pageantry, when the four Defence chiefs – Earl Mountbatten, Admiral Sir David Luce, General Sir Richard Hull and Air Chief Marshal Sir Charles Elsworthy, took their 20-minute spell in the death watch by the bier.

For two hours Churchill's contemporaries, friends and ex-foes alike, moved by. Peers and Commons, the Royal Household and foreign Ambassadors were the only figures on this momentous scene. For the first two hours of the lying-in-state, these people claimed Churchill for themselves. The Earl Marshal of England had decided that this unique moment was not for the history books. No reporters were allowed in. No record was made.

As Big Ben struck 11, fateful hour in two world wars, the physician who pronounced Sir Winston dead joined the VIP queue moving slowly across the silent, carpeted floor. Lord Moran was as much a friend as doctor to the man beneath the Union Jack. He walked, black topper in hand, explaining the scene to a grave-faced boy in grey. As the chimes of

Parliament's clock died away, the guard about the bier went about its silent change, every movement ordered by two smart raps from a scabbard on the stone floor. The flow of people on either side of the bier halted as the new guard took over. So, for a full minute, Lord Moran gazed at the bright Garter emblems resting on the coffin of his Knightly friend.

Throughout the day, policemen, strangely gentle, urged the twin flows along. By nightfall, as offices closed and the queue grew, they were passing through at the rate of 4,000 an hour. The interminable, anonymous stream flowed on through the night. Occasionally a famous face went slowly by. The Marquis of Exeter – Lord Burghley the athlete – limped steadily past the bier on two walking-sticks. Behind him came an unknown, grey-bearded man, a crucifix clutched to his chest.

Mothers carried sleeping babies. Small, uncomprehending boys clutched comics, and even tried to read them by the light of the tall candles. Always there were tears, women blowing their noses hard, men flicking away something that seemed to have got into the eye. But for everyone who cried there were a hundred who straightened their shoulders. It wasn't grief which invested Westminster Hall tonight, it was pride.

28 January 1965

The last salute from the captains and the kings

FROM THE MOSCOW RIVER to the Zambesi, from new nations he fashioned and old thrones he secured, they came to London at Churchill's last bidding, and not a prince or a prelate among them but was in his debt.

And, for all their history, the steps of St. Paul's have never framed as rich a tapestry as this. They poured from the West door behind his coffin and froze in the moment of farewell into a unique picture of majesty and power, a court summoned by Death to mourn the uncommon Commoner.

MULCHRONE'S BRITAIN

The Viking kings, Olav of Norway and Frederik of Denmark, were there, rugged old sailors saluting Royal Navy fashion. Constantine of Greece, handsome and dashingly cloaked, knowing better than most what his own throne owes to that corpse. Baudouin, King of the Belgians, still touchingly young among the greybeards, his own country so firmly bound to Churchill by sinews of war. Juliana of Holland and her gay consort, now both unnaturally grave.

Towering above them all, his mere presence a brave remembrance, stood Charles de Gaulle, Churchill's occasional adversary and his proudest ally. There he is, people whispered, and you knew without looking whom they meant. He threw up his high, elegant, St Cyr salute as the coffin was returned to the gun carriage and kept it there, this great cliff of a man, long after the others.

Princes of Sweden and Liechtenstein, Ethiopia and Luxemburg, the Presidents of Uruguay and Iceland, the Premiers of Britain and Canada, all with their eyes riveted on the flag-draped coffin.

All held back a little to give precedence to our own Royal Family, the Gloucesters, the Kents, the Princess Royal, who shook her head sadly at some personal memory as she watched the coffin disappear. Princess Margaret and her husband stood behind the Queen Mother and the Prince of Wales, who has become a tall, slim colt.

Before the Queen and Prince Philip, and holding upright the mourning sword of the City of London, jet black from point to hilt, the Lord Mayor performed the City's last service to its most illustrious freeman.

The frame of this rare picture was provided by members of the College of Arms, face cards from an historic pack in their quartered tabards. There was a surprising amount of colour in what at first glance looked a sombre scene of unrelieved black.

The tabards glowed scarlet and blue and old gold. There were glimpses of rich sashes beneath the billowing cloaks of King Constantine and Prince Bernhard.

And, for all this great throng, and for all the long minutes it took the coffin to regain the gun carriage, the silence was such that you could hear a single footfall in the heart of London.

When Churchill went the kings and the captains stood very still, like children trying to be good.

Then, as the gun carriage began to move, they snapped up a last salute. The spell broke. They seemed to shiver a little. They stamped their feet, and talked quietly among themselves.

A single Lightning shrieked overhead, reconnoitring the fly-past route.

'Achtung, Spitfire,' said a middle-aged man in the crowd. Some people around us nodded and smiled because he had packed a lot of memories into the two words.

To the people outside St Paul's Sir Winston's life had run its full, glorious span. If the day was sad, it was also brave, and the brave show, rather than the sombre, seemed to have more of Churchill in it.

He was in the proud banners of the Cinque Ports and the Arms of the Spencer Churchills. He was even more in the decorations that had been lavished upon him, now bright jewels and bold ribbons on beds of black velvet carried by four officers of the Queen's Royal Irish Hussars, the regiment with which his own amalgamated. But supremely he was in the symbols of the Garter, the one payment he accepted for saving his country and the one which went with him atop his coffin.

The Churchills, with that distinctive set of the jaw, walked behind, his son Randolph looking as if all the fire had gone out of him. Lady Churchill and the women of the family stepped from the five carriages loaned by the Queen. Mr Randolph Churchill took his mother's left arm in the crook of his right arm. Then he reached across with his left hand and grasped hers as if to secure it there.

Together they watched as the eight Guardsmen, hands as gentle as women's, pulled the coffin from the gun carriage and on to their shoulders. There was only a jingle of harness in the still air. The waiting pallbearers, Churchill's contemporaries in power, his advisers, his captains of war, turned on each flank to escort their old friend.

And none in all that brave scene showed more courage than the deathly frail, deathly pale old man to whom the coffin came first. Earl Attlee won the sympathy of countless thousands because it seemed he, at any rate, would go through with the funeral of his old chief even though it put his own life in hazard. But he saw it through. And when, at the end, the precedence of others kept him waiting for his car in the cold for 20 minutes, he did not complain.

A great clash of bells shouted that Churchill was going for the last time. The coffin tilted as it moved down the steps. Randolph Churchill saw his mother to her carriage. She walked very straight, and her short steps were firm. Her heavy veil hid Winston's 'Clemmie' from the world. The Navy took the strain on the ropes. The kings and the captains saluted. The man in the crowd said 'Achtung Spitfire.' And Churchill was gone.

1 February 1965

Chichester the wanderer returns

SIR FRANCIS CHICHESTER, navigator extraordinary to the Second Elizabethan age, rejoined the world at Plymouth tonight. He looked at it through his National Health specs and said: 'Oh dear.'

One could see his point. Plymouth, ecstatic, elated out of its somewhat puritan primness (the pubs were open pretty well all day) shattered his long, self-sought solitude with a roistering, boisterous welcome home. Its very massiveness emphasised the minuteness of the man – and of the sliver of a thing in which he had circumnavigated the globe.

Gipsy Moth IV danced into Plymouth's historic Sound looking as insignificant as the pilot boat of some scratch armada – so big was the fleet of vessels which had gone out to fuss over her homecoming.

At the breakwater 65-year-old Sir Francis was joined by Lady Chichester and his son Giles, who travelled ashore with him in the harbour master's barge after he had tied up.

But what awaited Sir Francis ashore was even more astonishing. The welcoming arms of the great bay, from Devil's Point in the west to Heybrook Bay in the east, were literally alive with people. They carpeted the Hoe from waves to summit. The only grass visible on the Hoe itself was where it was too precipitous for a handhold. Every ancient parapet, every modern prom, was jammed solid. They stood on high roofs, scrambled dangerously over rocks, they pressed along every pier, filled every small boat that could put to sea.

It was into this crazy scene that Chichester stepped calmly ashore. Braced with a glass of champagne, and taking his time to change into his favourite jacket, he stood a little unsteadily on the jetty. In answer to the Lord Mayor's greeting he said: 'I look back and think of the great sailors who have sailed from Plymouth, and to be reckoned among these is a great honour for me.' The massive crowd set up a rhythmic clapping, interspersed with cries of 'Francis, Francis'. They sang 'For he's a jolly good fellow.'

The Sound took on the look of some crazy regatta when two minutes before 9 pm the maroons sounded the rover's return across the breakwater. The sky seemed to blush with pleasure and brushed the water with golden light. Lady Chichester, in pillar-box red, climbed aboard Gipsy Moth IV and kissed her husband. Giles followed and embraced his father. With him he had brought two bottles of champagne.

Royal Marine inflatable dinghies skittered protectively around the ketch, keeping at bay the wild flotilla, its hundreds of navigation lights bobbing on the swell, which threatened to crush Gipsy Moth in her hour of triumph. A ten-gun salute from the Royal Artillery crashed out from the Citadel. A fire float spouted red, white and blue water. There was an explosion of sirens and cheers and whistles. When Gipsy Moth reached her buoy, a hundred yards off the jetty, the armada slewed to a halt and formed a massive, semi-circular jam of yachts, yawls, launches, tugs, dinghies, prams and even canoes.

The magnificent navigator who stepped ashore here tonight is cast in no heroic mould. What Plymouth and the world saw was a sparely built man of 65 badly in need of a haircut, a sensitive, cranky, introverted loner trying to stifle his embarrassment to please our landlubberly notion of what was an appropriate welcome.

Any distaste that might have been felt for the publicity machine, for the commercialism involved – the Chichester mugs, dishcloths and so on – or for the delusions of mock Elizabethan grandeur his feat has inspired, fell away as the stooping figure stepped ashore.

He did not seem immediately at ease. He was feeling, they said, that extra sensitivity which presses on a sailor after a long voyage. He looked back at his craft – which already looks as unreal, as incapable of the task it has performed, as those early space craft which have already been consigned to the international exhibition circuit.

Plymouth, which saw him off almost casually, spared neither time, trouble nor cash to welcome him back in a fine froth of Devonian pride. They had thought of everything – right down to two Marines to support him in case his sea legs betrayed him ashore after 119 days afloat (they didn't), and a hairdresser who waited for hours on end in the Guild Hall to trim his shaggy grey hair. Signal flags spelled out 'Welcome Francis' above the Royal Western Yacht Club, and the Hoe and every headland for miles around took up the message in the flags of all nations.

For two days the city's pubs had been open almost all day (with breaks for restocking the bars) and beer tents fringing the Hoe had been topping up topers tired of waiting. And it was a long wait – too long for those with small children.

For a time it seemed that he might not make it today. The light was already beginning to fade when they radioed Chichester from the yacht club for his decision. 'I'm coming in,' he said. On the Hoe a military band brayed and a beat group sang that it would overcome, and two tired little girls paraded a poster saying 'Hurry up, Sir Francis, we haven't slept for two days.'

And at last he came – nine months and a day after slipping down the Sound. But before the world whisked him off he turned once more towards his yacht, now almost shrouded in darkness, and raised his right hand in a half salute.

29 May 1967

'They'll know where Sunderland is now'

THAT'S NOT THE CUP the players' wives brought back to Sunderland last night, me bonny lad, it's the grail. Like no other place in Britain, Sunderland *needed* that pot as a symbol of pride and hope.

Grown men cried in the streets. They kissed their television sets. There hasn't been such an explosion in the town since a local called Mills invented a bomb.

Strangely, and sadly, it isn't just Cup fever. For Sunderland, unlike those euphoric headlines yesterday, is *not* Wunderland. This is a town were 40 lads queue for one job. Where boys go straight from school on to the dole. Some go south for work, like their grandfathers had to. But this is a place where a move two streets away is quite a wrench.

The Wearsiders are close-knit, tough, salt-of-the-earth people – and they've got seven and a half per cent unemployment.

The progress to Wembley was like a march to war. As lowly Sunderland smelled the scent of victory, production figures shot up at Wearmouth Colliery. Output went up at the shipyards. When the chairman of one yard said he reckoned this was '80 per cent due to exceptionally fine weather and 20 per cent to Bob Stokoe,' the Sunderland manager, most Wearsiders felt he'd got the figures the wrong way round.

Wearside desperately wants new industries. In this poster-plastered town (whole houses have disappeared behind red and white decorations) the most telling motto was 'Put Sunderland Back on the Map, Lads.'

The lads obliged. Long before Wembley, the town council thanked the team for what they were doing for Sunderland.

The Lord Mayor of arch-rivals Newcastle, soon to be joined administratively with Sunderland, sent his opposite number a telegram which said: 'The English Cup at Roker would be a good omen for the new Tyne and Wear authority.'

It was this pent-up need for recognition, for pride that never fully recovered from the cruel economic blow, the 30s, that exploded in Sunderland.

About the only all-white outfit you can buy in Sunderland just now is a Holy Communion dress. The shops seem to have nothing but red and white dresses, red and white skirts and sweaters, red and white Y-fronts, red and white pushchairs.

On Saturday morning there were red and white ribbons around dog collars, teddy bears and the hair curlers of old women who had never seen a football match in their lives. Even a bridal car sported red and white ribbons.

'And they ordered a TV set for the reception,' said the chauffeur.

Some of the pubs closed at 2 pm – to give bar staffs a chance to watch the match on TV, said the landlords. The customers took a different view. As one said: 'If they'd tried to shut at three, with the game starting, it would have taken a battalion of the DLI (the Durham Light Infantry) to get us out.'

Fred Lowther put two strangers out of his pub, the Blandford. 'I know all the rest,' said Fred, a 45-year-old magistrate. 'And I know there'll be no trouble.'

There was no trouble, just pandemonium. They hardly had time to order their ale in case they missed a move. Nobody heard a word of commentary for the chanting, the yells of 'Howay, Lads'. The agonised yells when Leeds looked dangerous.

MULCHRONE'S BRITAIN

It was only a TV set, but they waved their scarves at it and screamed encouragement at individual players.

Fred Lowther donned a faded red and white cap with a tattered tassel. 'My grandfather wore this at Wembley when we won in 1937, and it is going to bring us luck.' A thoughtful man. Passionate about his home town. He said: 'We've been in the doldrums so long with our unemployment, our social problems and so on – but this has given the kiss of life to the town.' He is too practical a businessman to imagine that industry will now flock to Sunderland. 'But it might well have an indirect effect,' he added hopefully.

Now the whole pub knew the Almighty wears a red and white shirt, and Bob Stokoe is his Messiah.

As the second-half minutes ticked by with unbearable slowness, one rugged customer asked Fred Lowther to unlock the pub door and release him from the tension.

The street, all the streets were deserted. In the furniture store the staff were in the armchairs watching the match. In the carpet shop the assistants sprawled on the carpets, eyes glued to a portable TV.

Then, suddenly, if only for a little while, the town was Wunderland.

Until four in the morning, or until felled by drink or exhaustion, they went crazy. They threw street parties for the kids, just like VE Day. They danced round the Cenotaph, they snaked chanting and singing, faces glazed, through the streets. Car horns made the night hideous. Tapping out the message 'We Are The Champions.'

Perfect strangers embraced each other – definitely not a Wearside trait. I was watching the girls dancing in their stockinged feet in the window of the bakery in Market Square when Leonard Meek, a 37-year-old warehouse worker, shook my hand for no other reason than his overbrimming happiness.

'Ah cried, me bonny lad,' he said.

'Ah couldn't help it. You tell 'em in London about us. They'll know where Sunderland is now.'

The Cup arrived last night.

Today the Youth Employment Office in Gray Road opened its doors to the inevitable queue.

7 May 1973

By rickshaw through Southampton

SIGN OF THE TIMES, I suppose, Carruthers, but Britain now has its first rickshaw service. And the coolie, damme, is a white man. To be accurate, it's a trishaw – a bicycle up front and seats for two behind. Apart from the fact that it is clean, it is no different from a couple of million or so which are the taxis of the poor, eastward from the Persian Gulf to San Francisco, where motor-cars start again. And its coolie – sorry, operator – doesn't do it for a bowl of rice a day, spitting betel juice all over the streets of Southampton.

Spitting in the street in Southampton is against the law. So, for all anybody knows, is operating a trishaw at 25p for any reasonable journey in the city centre. Southampton's transport committee have wisely turned a blind, Nelsonian eye to the nation's first trishaw, at least until they have studied the fine print of the Hackney Carriage laws.

It is also possible that they are slightly bemused by the trishaw wallah, Mr Rob Lakin. Mr Lakin is a sane, respectable, 26-year-old chemical engineer who plies for hire only in his spare time. What's bemusing is why he does it at all. 'It was an idea,' he says. 'And as we have only about 70 years to live, I believe we should leap at ideas. I don't want to die of mediocrity. Cycling is a very lonely way to travel, but this isn't. We talk about cars polluting the air. Well, this is a positive way to pollute nothing. Then again, there isn't exactly a lot of fun about, is there? And this is fun.'

It's true. Wherever he pedalled me in Southampton people smiled at the sight. Grown men shouted childish things like: 'Your front wheel's going round, mister,' and others made uncouth remarks about Mr Lakin's efforts to move what is usually my personal weight problem.

But then, no stay-at-home Briton has ever seen man transporting man by muscle power. You'd have to be a fair old age to remember the Bath chairs at Bournemouth. Whereas I have travelled in rickshaws from Dehra Dun to Bandoeng, not to mention Honkers, Rangers, Bangers and Singapoops.

MULCHRONE'S BRITAIN

I have watched the memsahibs of Calcutta, parasols aflutter, use rickshaws in a manner that lent them the dignity of a brougham. I must have been a pretty soppy sort of sahib, because I always wound up feeling sorry for the rickshaw wallah, to the extent of stopping him short of my destination and then over-tipping. Oh, they stick out their puny chests when they tout for your patronage. But, once in the high seat, you look down on the skinny little devil, every minute muscle straining, legs that wouldn't hold a tomato plant, and spitting betel juice like a consumptive *in extremis.*

Above Dehra Dun there's a hill station called Mussoorie, where the Raj built its first brewery for the troops, and where Sunday dinner to this day is still roast beef and Yorkshire pud. The main street of Mussoorie is such a switchback that it takes four men to handle a rickshaw – two pulling uphill and two on ropes behind acting as brakes downhill. The overmanning problem makes any journey expensive, and the terrain makes you seasick.

There are retired Zulu rickshawmen in Durban who frighten their young with tales of the Royal Navy's way with their rickshaws. One befeathered Zulu could pull any four average tars on a tour of the lovely city's bars. The horror began when the drunken tars put the Zulu in his own rickshaw and raced other rickshaws, pulled by other sailors, back to the jetty. In Zulu history, those races rank pretty close to what happened at Rorke's Drift.

Saigon used to be made hideous by the noise of motorised trishaws, the best known of which was topped by a six-foot-high fan stolen from an office and worked from the engine. The delightful thing about it was that its draught was aimed not at his perspiring passengers, but at the driver.

We have not yet reached such sophistication in Southampton, though Mr Lakin is having a hood made for his passengers against the return of traditional British weather.

He sees trishaws spreading. 'I don't want to become a trishaw tycoon,' he said. 'But these things would be wonderful in parks or on seaside promenades.'

A passing policeman chipped in. 'Why,' he said, 'don't you do regular tours around places of historic interest in the city? A lot of people would go for that.'

But Mr Lakin wasn't listening. He was looking out over the sparkling calm of Southampton Water. He had just leapt at another idea. When he came out of his reverie it was to ask: 'Wouldn't that be a smashing place for a gondola?'

16 June 1975

PORTRAIT GALLERY

She looks nothing, is nothing, except a Saint

IT IS NOT EVERY DAY that Cobham, Surrey, has a Saint pop in for a cup of tea and a chat. Her saintliness apart, Mother Teresa is probably the only woman to be given a motor-car by the Pope.

It was the enormous, white Lincoln Continental given the Holy Father to use at the Bombay Eucharistic Congress. When he left India he left the car to an obscure nun in a Calcutta slum – Mother Teresa. 'I felt too shy even to stand near it,' she told me yesterday. She used it for the only practical purpose she has for cars. 'We heard there was a child dying of starvation in the street. I sent a couple of sisters in the car to bring him in.'

Then, being a severely practical Saint, she flogged it for a grossly inflated £15,000 to a rich Hindu who wanted to bask in its slightly sanctified glory. She took it half in cash, half in buildings – all for her work.

She is a little woman of 54 with a craggy, parchment face and deep, sad eyes which she can light with a toothy grin. She is an Albanian who talks English with the 'Bombay Welsh' lilt. She was dressed in what amounted to about 5s. worth of teacloths, a blue edged sari of the cheapest muslin. A safety-pin held the crucifix at her left shoulder. Two straight pins kept the head-dress straight on her shaven head.

She looks nothing, is nothing, except a Saint – a notion she rejects with comic disbelief.

They don't share her disbelief in the howling, pestilential slums of Calcutta, where, for 14 years, Mother Teresa has been performing one of the most remarkable works of Christian charity on the face of the earth. She succours the destitute dying – an empty phrase for the monstrously sickening task of picking starving wrecks from the stinking gutters of the city and easing their last hours with a little milk and rice, and love.

'There was a little baby the other day,' she said. 'It couldn't have been four days old. Its mother had wrapped it in a newspaper and abandoned it under a seat in a bus. Oh, that's a favourite place. Or in a rickshaw. Or in a dustbin. The poor people. They have no food for them.

'Or there was the man, starving, who cried for food as they carried him in. He was too far gone to eat any. I gave him a little milk. Next morning we gave him the first plate of rice he had seen for a long time.

'He dug his two hands into it and tried to stuff it into his mouth. But he never got it because in that moment he fell dead.'

Mother Teresa's expressive hands were at work, trying to stuff the imaginary rice into her own mouth, as if the words could not convey all the horror by themselves.

She looked around the little group of Surrey matrons, in summer hats and pearls, to see if the memory from the smell and sweat of Calcutta was making sense in the quiet, antiseptic convent room in the cool, evergreenery of Surrey. She had come to thank *them*, to promise them her prayers for the raffles they had organised and the Christmas cards they had sold, and the money they had sent.

She is a living, and very practical legend, from the Himalayas to Ceylon, from West Bengal to Kerala – the Saint of the Gutters, where the hopeless lie down to die. The hands she used so expressively yesterday are more used to cleaning the filth from starving near-corpses, to coaxing a few to live a little longer, to giving to those who can't a straw mattress and a blanket and encouragement to make peace with whichever God they are about to meet.

'Castes and creeds mean nothing to us,' she said. 'The Hindus come at 2.30 every day to take their dead to the burning ghats. The Mohammedans collect their own. It doesn't matter that they are not of my faith. They are all Christ come in disguise. *"I was homeless and you took me in."*

'A Saint? Oh no – except in so far as we are all saints, as St Paul said.'

As her fame spread, so did Mother Teresa's responsibilities.

What started as a lonely work is now an Order – The Missionaries of Charity – with 250 sisters. Mostly Indians, but with some Germans, Americans and Maltese, they are spread throughout India, caring for the dying, feeding and teaching orphans, organising lepers into viable communities.

She is on her way to answer a call from the Bishops of Venezuela. The four nuns with her will found a branch of the Order in the slums of that country of great riches and hideous poverty.

The five arrived in England with just £3 each in their pockets. Mother Teresa's worldly goods did not strain the capacity of two faded khaki knitting bags.

'I must go,' she said. 'The poverty there is as bad as it is in Calcutta. And who knows' – with a smile as close to being crafty as a Saint can come – 'who knows, with our presence there, the rich may even come to know that the poor exist.'

22 July 1965

The most surprising story I've written

DOWN FROM THE COOLINS, cursing the weather in the old tongue – *Tha e fluich an diugh* – comes a card-carrying member of the Scottish Nationalist Party, a bronzed mountain man with a hint of salt herring on his breath. Meet Abdul Kaliq, man of Skye.

While the barman poured him his dram he looked down at the barman's McKinnon kilt and offered to get him a new one at a fiercely competitive price.

'Hey, I've got some great terylene hipsters.'

There was no response from the men steaming in wet serge. He tried the housekeeper. 'Hey, Mary, how about some Arran wool? Best in the world. B– all to do in winter but knit.' Nobody bought. Anyway, Kaliq wasn't really trying, just keeping his hand in. He misses the bazaar at Lahore.

When he sold the hotel proprietor a pair of gumboots at the regulation price of 70s. he was unhappy about it for a week.

The proprietor knew something was amiss when Kaliq tried to press a quarter-bottle of whisky on him. Then the Pakistani blurted it out. 'Look, when I say 70s., you're not supposed to give me 70s., just like that. You're supposed to say "Sixty shillings," and we argue from there.'

Skye, somewhat to its surprise, has just about the best-integrated Pakistani in Britain. It had another, but he left a few days ago.

Says Kaliq: 'When they called him "black bastard" it hurt him inside. When they call me "black bastard" I call them "white bastard," and we have a drink. If that's integration, then I'm well integrated.'

He came here ten years ago with nothing but a suitcase, a packman selling drapery and shoes on tick, lugging the heavy case around the high crofts, anywhere to make a sale.

Now he owns a busy, bulging store, where you can buy an ice-cream or a suit at ten o'clock at night.

He has a plump, laughing Skye woman for his wife, and three sloe-eyed children who are being brought up in the Church of Scotland. Well-mannered children, too, cared for as they are by an experienced nanny, Miss Katie McDonald, who has served nobility.

Kaliq sometimes laughs at the huge improbability of it all. 'Feller tells me the other week his gross takings were £120 a week. I said, "Man, that wouldn't keep my kids in lollipops".' He dotes on the children. 'They eat porridge. I stick to curry. They say, "Daddy, your food tastes funny".'

Says the schoolmaster, primly: 'It really is most extraordinary the way he has settled down.' The hotel proprietor is more certain. 'He is probably the most popular man on the island, and certainly the best known.'

Kaliq meant to settle in Glasgow, humping his suitcase round the tenements. 'But those people – they'd take something on credit and when you went back for the money they'd swear they'd never seen you in their lives. Here, they're very honest and very kind. They know I give 'em best bargain.'   •

It has not gone unnoticed that though Kaliq sells women's Wellingtons to tourists for 35s. a pair, he lets the island women have them for 27s. 6d.

He is a meticulous attender of 'Wee Free' funerals. Usually he knows about them before most people, for he leaves his wife in charge of the store and travels the island daily in his mobile shop. On mountain roads as steep and wild as his own Khyber, he has driven every mile of the island from Rubha Hunish to Ardavasar, from Milovaig to Kyleakin.

He had to learn the Gaelic to communicate – *Ciamar tha thu?* (How are you?) and *Te tha sin?* (How much is that?). Now, under Miss McDonald's tuition, he can hold a conversation. Nobody slips into the Gaelic to put one over on him.

He loves the nature of the place, the baby seals, the cormorants and shag, the eider duck and black guillemot. And he is lyrical about the views over Cruachan Beinn a' Chearcaill and Beinn nan Braclaich.

He is 32, and handsome, and laughs a lot with flashing teeth. To a newcomer in the bar he calls 'Hey, Jamie how about some new shirts?' Says Jamie: 'The last lot I got from you went yellow.'

Kaliq scarcely pauses.

'Got some new ones now that don't go yellow.' But he wasn't really trying.

His generosity is something of a legend. When a boy died recently and everybody sent flowers, Kaliq sent a basket of groceries for the funeral tea. Such news travels on the Island.

'They are my kind of people,' he says, thoughtfully.

'They don't give me any trouble. I don't cause any. They know they can depend on me. Sometimes it's "black bastard". I don't mind. I can deal with that. I don't run away. Business doing well. Got a good wife, lovely kids. I'm happy. I've applied for British citizenship. When I get that I'll be happier still.'

Abdul Kaliq, Scottish Nationalist, businessman extraordinary, looked far across the soaring heights of his unlikely kingdom, and laughed.

'Yes,' he said, 'I think Kaliq will stay.'

Just one thing more.

After we had parted I met a bank official from the mainland who was on his way to meet his valued client.

'I have to,' he said. I did not understand. 'Oh,' he said. 'Didn't you know? He can neither read nor write.'

21 October 1967

Chevalier – 'In private he spoke better English than I'

HE WAS A YEAR OLDER THAN the Eiffel Tower and, in British eyes, a more enduring monument to France. Maurice Chevalier was one of the immortals. Look around, Chaplin is left. Name the others.

There have been better French singers, certainly better actors, but Chevalier uniquely captured his British audience with his characterisation of a Frenchman who hasn't existed, if ever he truly did, since the Twenties.

Take his line from *Gigi*: 'Thang evenn for leedle gurrls.' In private, Chevalier spoke better English than I. But he clung to the character of the *boulevardier* of the Twenties until the end.

Before *Gigi* was mooted, and he was rising 70 then, he told me solemnly that he was planning *the* farewell tour. It wasn't, of course. He practically began a new career in films or, rather, a second one. The signed photographs on his study walls told some of the story. There was a 'Hi' from a youthful Bing Crosby, 'Regards' from Chaplin, 'Love' from Ingrid Bergman.

He was careful with his money. Part proof was the Utrillo securely clamped to an easel in the hall of his exquisite home in Marnes-la-Coquette, just outside Paris. He liked to say he learned his thrift from Harry Lauder. 'I knew them all,' he would say. 'Jack Buchanan, Sid Field, Al Jolson, Lupino Lane...'

But, before them, he knew Mistinguett and Josephine Baker at the Folies Bergeres in the early Thirties. And Douglas Fairbanks and Mary Pickford. They all helped him. He always spoke of them with some awe.

It was perhaps part affectation, but certainly part of the man, that he could never believe his luck. Planning that 'last' tour, he would say to me 'If I am lucky enough to make a hit...' or 'If I am a success in London...'

He was a sort of Parisian toff forever paying tribute to his 'Cockney' background. The son of a house painter, he earned his first franc at 13 singing in the Café des Trois Lions in the scruffy suburb of Monilmontant. He went back often. One of his horrors was that some old friend should think him a 'tête montée', a big head.

In fact, the famous straw hat remained a modest 6⅝. He bought them six at a time, from a firm in Luton, Bedfordshire, where they make boaters for Harrow.

He was wounded and taken prisoner in the First World War (when he learned his English from an officer in the Durham Light Infantry) and was cleared of a charge of collaboration in the Second.

We remember him for songs like *Mimi* and *Valentine* and *I'm glad I'm not young any more.*

The French remember him for quite different songs, starting with *Madelon de la Victoire,* an expression of French *gloire* after 1918, *Chapeaux* and *Les Pas Perdus.*

By 1930 he could earn £4,000 a week in London and £1,000 merely for singing at a private party.

He married once – Yvonne Vallee, in 1927. They were divorced in 1933. He had his affaires though he wasn't the womaniser his stage character suggested.

When he came to London last March to launch his autobiography *I remember it well* he said: 'There is a woman to whom I am devoted, so I am very lucky. To finish without the hand of a woman near you is a sad way to end one's life.

'It is fine to be alone when you are younger. Better, perhaps. But not at the end. Then you must have a woman close to you...'

Let us hope that she was.

3 January 1972

Charlie becomes a suede-shoe knight

THE OLD CLOWN in his wheelchair bowed his head as far as his years would let him, which was not very far. When he raised his eyes to the Queen's smile, the kid from the wrong side of the Thames had been dubbed everybody's parfit, gentle knight, Sir Charles Chaplin.

For the first time in his 85 years he had been felicitously upstaged by a longer-running show called the monarchy, which didn't hesitate to borrow some of his old tricks. It is very rare, in my experience, that a formal setting, a crowd, and ceremonial meld to create a sensitive experience greater than the sum of the parts, but it happened for Charlie Chaplin in Buckingham Palace yesterday.

The string orchestra of the Welsh Guards had been hinting at it from the minstrel's gallery of the lofty ballroom when, during the long wait for the Queen, it inserted, into selections from light opera, Chaplin's own music from *The Countess from Hong Kong*.

When the Queen was just two minutes away, the orchestra fell silent, leaving the pianist, a sergeant, to play, solo, Chaplin's *Smile... Though your Heart is Aching*. And when the call 'Sir Charles Chaplin' rang out, the musicians switched effortlessly, but with moving effect, into his theme music from *Limelight*. It may just be fancy that, as a palace steward wheeled the old man to stage centre, 1,000 people were silently humming I'll be loving you eternally...' But I know I was.

Charlie had hoped to be able to walk the 10 yards to the Queen, and kneel with his right knee on the plush stool. As it was, he managed to bow his white head, with its little tonsure. The Queen tapped him, first on his right shoulder, then the left, with the sword her father used as Colonel-in-Chief of the Scots Guards (for the simple reason that it is lighter than any of the others).

For him she had that smile which dims whole chandeliers and Charlie Chaplin, as he later recalled, was 'dumbfounded'. But the quick mind in the slow old body remembered: 'She thanked me for all that I had done. She said my films had helped her a great deal.'

The new Sir Charles was in morning dress, but indulged his fancy by wearing midnight blue suede shoes and carrying an Irish blackthorn stick. He also revealed a little, understandable, vanity by asking that no television shots should be taken of him climbing laboriously into the Daimler which took him back to the Savoy and a small round of parties given by old friends.

Asked how he was going to celebrate, he replied: 'Get drunk.' His wife gave a small shake of her head, for which he kissed her on both cheeks.

After his own dubbing he was wheeled unobtrusively into a position in front of the front row of guests, but to one side, out of the sight of most. Inescapably, it was the position a movie director would be in if cameras had been trained on the royal show.

Inescapably, it was the stiff, formal scene he could, one day, have sent up beautifully as he watched the crocodile of gallant, worthy, and eminently faceless people who keep bits of the country working, pass before the Queen to receive their reward.

(A gleam signalling heaven knows what clownish thought came into his eyes when, in the middle of the solemnity, the bandmaster's music stand collapsed with a clatter, though the band struggled on.)

With only a slight effort of imagination, it seemed as if the old wizard of comedy was nodding approval of the scene, of his principal lady, flanked by the flummery of her Yeomen of the Guard, her rigid Gurkha orderlies, the officers who made meticulously sure that the correct insignia, the right medal, went to the right man or woman, clear down to the lance corporal who was last in line.

The National Anthem froze the scene. The Queen, in a pale blue satin striped dress, turned to go, paused and directed a personal smile to the old clown in the wheel-chair.

She had honoured scores of her subjects. She had spent as much time chatting with the lance corporal as with anyone else. But she left the impression that she, too, knew that it was Charlie Chaplin's day at Buckingham Palace.

5 March 1975

THE ROYAL FAMILY

There are no Durbars any more

Mulchrone was known as the master-reporter of royal occasions. He enjoyed them, understood them and was never sycophantic to the royals he admired. The royal tour of Australia and New Zealand in 1963 was a tricky one. Its success was a good deal in doubt beforehand and this brought out the best in him.

ME WHITE MAN. Queen, she white woman. New Zealanders they various attractive shades of brown. And if I hear one more suntanned subject moaning that the Queen looks pale, wan and tired, I swear I'll deport him to an English winter.

The Queen, I have it on what might be described as the only possible authority, is in fact having a ball. Short of spelling it out, I cannot more plainly refute the snide hinting by some news agencies that this royal tour is a bit of a flop. Another canard best got out of the way says that the crowds which greet her are not as big as they might be, nor the welcome as great. By any test this is just not true.

The Queen's policy on this tour is 'Don't call on me, I'll call on you.' And the tour organisers here have co-operated down to such details as publishing route maps of the Queen's road journeys so that a farmer and his family might see her the more intimately at their own crossroads without the fuss and expense of going into town.

The crowds, thick enough in the towns, have been more dispersed. The abiding impression of this royal progress to date has been one of family groups sipping lemonade outside crossroads stores. Father has his son and heir on his shoulders, at the risk of losing an eye every time the lad waves his flag. Mother hasn't bothered to change out of her workaday floral print, and baby in the push-chair looks as though she's going to spoil it all by being sick at the crucial moment.

There are no Durbars any more. There are crossroads and kids. That is how it should be. That is how it is.

Would you wait in your thousands in a drizzle on a road outside Manchester for the briefest glimpse of the Queen? They did last night here in Wellington. As for affection, I have never seen it more patently and movingly expressed.

An effort this, for the New Zealanders are more po-faced than we are. They are the only people I've struck who offer you a welcoming drink with a look of sorrowful concern. They are the most straight-laced and straight-faced of the South Sea islanders, yet they opened their hearts to the Queen in a manner which should put us to shame. Their cheers, like ours, sound half-hearted, but aren't. Their waves are every bit as tentative.

Like us they sing *God Save the Queen* only as long as the fellow next door starts it. In a word, they suffer from a bad case of being British,

But there is one subtle exception, and that perhaps the most vital factor of the Queen's whole tour.

After the restrained, loyal cheers have died, there lingers an air almost of disenchantment. As one charming, loyal and intelligent woman put it to me today: 'We feel we are being patronised.' Not, mark you, by the Queen. But an uneasy current runs beneath this royal tour, one which says that the Mother Country was ready to sell New Zealand up the River Seine before the Bailiff of that particular water lowered the boom.

In New Zealand, Queen or no Queen, there is no escaping the Common Market. The external symbols and the deepest loyalties are British, but it would be dangerous for the stranger to make the obvious assumptions. The pipe band playing *'Bonnie Dundee'* on the sands has its back not to the North Sea but to the South Pacific Ocean.

The milk bar has meat pie and chips on the menu and the Archers on the radio, but the more far-seeing of its customers are already thinking in terms of increased trade with Japan and other countries of their own ocean.

I have made a point of meeting the more disenchanted New Zealanders in the alleyways of four-ale bars (which in this otherwise glorious country still close at 6 pm.). I make no excuses, for bars are where voters are. And the voters say things like: 'You've let us down. You'll sell us out the minute it suits you. You never stood alone in 1940, because we were always with you. We stayed on short rations long after the war to feed you. You've sent the Queen here to placate us because you thought that by this time you'd be in the Common Market.' This is a composite view and the

75

latter notion, apparently widely held, doesn't, to my thinking, bear sane scrutiny. But the emotions are both real and disquieting. New Zealand knows that it stands at a crossroads in its history.

13 February 1963

Hobart breathes a bit heavily

THERE WAS A MOMENT TO SAVOUR TODAY... An official dashed into the mayor's parlour in Hobart town hall and addressed the lord mayor, aldermen and all their ladies: 'For Gawd's sake, get out – they're ruddy well here.'

And here, in fact, they ruddy well were, driving down the main street towards the town hall nine minutes ahead of schedule.

They call Hobart 'Slowbart.'

But not from today.

They were all in their appointed places on the platform when the Queen's Rolls stopped, albeit breathing a little heavily. If Her Majesty mistook this for an excess of emotion, well, how was she to know it was just so many incipient coronaries?

Hobart, praise be, is different. (In the hall of the Royal Hobart Golf Club a notice chalked on a blackboard read: 'Beware 4ft black snake in rough between 9th tee and 14th fairway. Kill on sight!')

Hobart, with its old brownstone buildings in a magnificent setting of sea and hills, is Lytham-sur-Mer, a Rivieran Weymouth. A gem of the Southern Seas – with chips and peas.

There's none of the Ascot hat nonsense of Adelaide and Melbourne about Hobart. The family groups along the royal route today could have been out shopping for socks on Manchester's Market Street.

The colours are drabber, the wind cooler. In fact, when the Queen drove up through the clouds to the 4,000ft summit of Mount Wellington it was decidedly nippy. She put on the first overcoat she has worn since she left England. And the breeze whipped out the Duke's tie, revealing – should you be a student of these things – a Dior label.

Apart from showing her some of the bonny children thrashing around in their Olympic swimming pool, that was about all the people of Hobart asked of the Queen today.

They took her up their mountain to show her one of the great panoramas of the world – the gentle mountains, the lovely headlands along the broad River Derwent, and Hobart, Australia's second oldest city, spread out at her feet.

It was hazy and clouds forming around the mountain slopes below interfered with the view, but still it was a grand scene, more moving than any number of loyal addresses.

28 February 1963

The 'Kwine' and her critics

IN ONE OF SYDNEY'S brassier boozers I asked my neighbour: 'What do you think of the royal tour?' His reply caused frozen beer to start steaming in four bars on two floors and, for the first time in human memory, made an Australian barmaid blush.

Five minutes later he stood beside me outside the pub, gentle as a lamb, waving to the Queen. There is only an apparent, not a real, paradox here. After all, if the Australian can't feel uncomfortable about royal tours, love the Queen, think the Duke a bit of a lad, and carry on his love-hate relationship with Britain in his own sweet way then what the hell's the point of paying taxes?

This tour, perhaps because of the paradoxes it has thrown up, has been a success. The Jeremiahs, the cynics, have largely been those who have closed their minds, inside the bar, and haven't bothered to see what was happening outside on the pavements.

I repeat, the tour has been a success. And I say this in the knowledge that Australians have stayed away in droves. Given a public holiday, sunshine, and the chance of a picnic with the kids on a beach just ten minutes away, the population of, say, Huddersfield would do exactly the same. Yet I don't see Republicanism ravaging Huddersfield.

An average Australian's approach (and I have his name and address should any tribunal ever need it) was: 'I took the kids to see her on the corner of the street because I feel they should. And for the rest of the time I watched her on television with a beer in my hand.'

Does that attitude make the tour a flop? Or doesn't it, rather, make it more typically British?

There was no television in Australia when the Queen was last here in 1954. And television, whatever its virtues, does not make for crowds on royal routes.

The affection of the Australians for their Queen, 1963 being what it is, is a startling, and sometimes even a humbling, thing. The most massive tribute, as always, has come from the crowds, the massive, unidentified, uninterviewed crowds who *didn't* go to the beach, who didn't entirely trust the telly, but who stood in the sun for hours to get one glimpse of the 'Kwine.'

They have been her best critics. She doesn't smile enough. (She doesn't.) She doesn't unbend to children. (She never pats, fondles, or even touches one.)

They don't know quite what they want of a queen any more than we do. The popular cry is that she should mix more, and more obviously, with 'ordinary people'. In spite of her express wish, the local Establishment has frequently seen to it that she doesn't.

But, really, no one knows what to expect of the confrontation of an ancient monarchy with the forms and feelings of this day and age. The Queen offered a hopeful pointer by giving a series of zippy lunch parties aboard Britannia, at which her guests included champion swimmers, school prefects, hurdlers, authors and racing men. But the people *will* have their circuses.

Oh, they want the Queen all right. But they're not quite sure *how* they want her any more than we are. But that they should want her and, by extension, want us, will suit me.

22 March 1963

Unabashed, they took over the proceedings

HER ROYAL HIGHNESS THE BRIDE – I cannot better the compliment – looked as beautiful as her mother. Angus Oglivy was patently the happiest man in the Abbey. The rest is commentary. This couple have no need of superlatives. They *were* superlative. Their happiness in each other lit the old stones, dimmed the lights of the monster called TV, put pomp in its place.

Hedged about by history, hemmed in by every known degree of royalty, baked by arc lights, and gobbled up by zoom lenses, the Princess and her groom were in a spot from which the Holy Ghost Himself might have shied away.

In the event, the Sacrament shone most serenely about this joyful couple. It was not the mighty resource of monarchy, or the platitudinous pomp of a great church which lifted this ceremony to a memorable peak. It was the joy of Alex and Angus.

The Abbey obviously enough, perhaps – has not married a couple who are so patently of the 60s. Whether *you* like it or not, the jargon has it that they are a couple who are 'with it'. And in so far as the phrase means an awareness of what is truly important in life, Alex and Angus really were with it yesterday.

Cool and unabashed, they pretty well took over the proceedings.

They spoke their lines with... yes, with fervour. Subtly, they made it clear that this was their day, their happiness, their Sacrament.

They smiled their joy right at the great, challenging head of the Archbishop of Canterbury. And His Grace of Canterbury just had to smile back. (As it was his first wedding in the Abbey he probably welcomed the opportunity.) Anyway, it was as if the North Foreland had broken into a grin.

CHAPTER FIVE

It was Angus who started it, of course. Angus, whose features are not as craggy as his photographs make out. Angus, who actually enjoys laughing and who, when he laughs, lets the thing go from ear to ear.

Feeling several million eyes upon him, and casting around for a friendly face in his first seconds in the Abbey, he turned to his family. They sat on white-and-gilt chairs (borrowed from St James's Palace) in the sacrarium, three ranks of Scottish nobility of a lineage which can look upon many of Europe's royal houses as so many Johnny-come-lately property developers. (And possibly would, were they not in business themselves.)

Angus, because of the geography of the seating arrangements, must have felt like one of those Jacobites who, temporarily and uneasily, found his fortune resting among Continental nobility. Anyway, he flashed the family a pair of raised eyebrows and a smile which clearly said: *'HELP'*.

Boldly into the breach of confidence stepped his best man, Mr Peregrine Fairfax, a red-headed farmer who looks as though he's a bit of a goer. The joke was obviously a good one. The groom resumed his natural jauntiness. The relief of tension continued for several minutes, interrupted by the passing of various royal processions.

At the passing of each, the groom and best man pulled themselves together, like naughty boys who've been told: 'Wipe that smile off your face,' and bowed their heads to Angus' processing in-laws.

The groom, of course, couldn't resist a sideways squint down the aisle. What he saw evidently shook him so much that he anticipated his cue by several seconds, and stepped out to wait for Princess Alexandra. For all that, they didn't really look at each other until long after the fanfares had died away and an anguishing anticipatory stillness had settled on the church.

The Dean of Westminster has one of the clearest, best-modulated voices in Christendom. He was also wearing the wine red cope (a very young Beaujolais, less than a year old) made for the Coronation of Charles II just 302 years and one day before, and one of his church's treasures. It was the Dean who declaimed the form of the Solemnisation of Matrimony, and he had not got further than the words 'to join together this man and this woman' when the Princess and her man exchanged the first of many smiles which excluded all the world.

This was the smile which made the whole thing sparkle. This was the point at which Alex and Angus took over. The Archbishop addressed the groom. Or, rather he intoned, with what I am sure was meant to be a reassuring smile: 'Angus...'

The bold Angus returned him a smile of such confident happiness that the older man couldn't fail to broaden his own.

And, suddenly, everybody relaxed, knowing it was going to be all right. In fact, Angus went a bit ahead of himself, and tried to jump the gun on 'for richer, for poorer'. The Archbishop, still smiling, steadied him.

Then the bride added her own joy. When she said '...thee Angus, to my wedded husband,' she turned to him, as if they were alone, and gave him a look he'll probably remember the day he dies. And I don't think it was merely my fancy that she bore down firmly on the words *and to obey*. Anyway, Angus looked mighty pleased.

The Archbishop has his own 'A'. He said 'end thereto I plight thee my troth.' Angus said 'and thereto...' with a long 'a' of his own. Oh, there was no doubt whose wedding it was.

Not that Angus lacked support. He had all the bonnie hoose o' Airlie there for a start. He had his char there, and his office messenger. Even his dentist. Few royal grooms of recent years have had so many good friends at their back.

Even so, the historical cockpit must have been pretty terrifying. Pitt was giving a frozen wave at the sacrarium steps. Peel sneered. David Garrick peeped from between his stone curtains. The nave and transepts were a garden of all those giddy colours brought out only by weddings – or Ascot.

All this, and Angus Ogilvy – if I judge him aright – dying for nothing more than a bit of peace and quiet and a cigarette. Or, if the in-laws are looking, a pipe.

But then came Princess Alexandra, with that crookedly winning smile. And all the weight fell away from Angus Ogilvy's shoulders.

Then, as I have said, they smiled at each other. And, from that moment on, all the Abbey's kings and queens, dead and alive, all the silly hats and the bored politicians, all the cameras, yes, and all we scribbling gawpers, might never have been there.

Some among us might have been seized by the sense of State occasion, overborne by living majesty, dazzled by cope and mitre, deafened senseless by organ and trumpet.

But not Alexandra and Angus. Alexandra and Angus were there just to get wed.

And that, most beautifully, they did.

25 April 1963

Just what do you want for the money, Willie?

WITH A LITTLE REFLECTION (and a lot of history) in mind, I find it a splendid thing that Mr William Hamilton (Lab, Fife W) can stand up in the Commons and lay into the Royal Family. But I am astonished that our Wullie, a considerable tactician, made the cardinal error of attacking possibly the most popular woman in the land and I wouldn't except the Sovereign – the Queen Mum herself.

Some of Mr. Hamilton's barbs went home. But he was way off target when he criticised the Queen Mother's rate for the job. He should have known he was on a good hiding to nothing when he criticised a Queen Dowager perhaps unique in British history, a character who has firmly and fondly imprinted her charm on the public imagination.

I can pinpoint her magic in one sentence. A member of 'A' Division of the Metropolitan Police guard (and who are allowed their private feelings about the 'Royals') said: 'When she smiles, she means it.'

After a youth orchestra performance she will meet the chosen few and then gently, but firmly, scythe her way through the ranks to meet the lads in the back row.

At the London Press Club the other night, an Irish member told her that they first met 20 years before, and she didn't look a day older. At 71, she blushed. 'You've kissed the Blarney Stone,' she said. She was to have stayed an hour. She stayed two and a half.

It has been well said that if the Queen Mum didn't exist, it would have been necessary to invent her. She knows we call her the 'Queen Mum,' and chuckles about it.

I see her, occasionally, racing at Lingfield. In her sheepskin jacket, she is as incognito as could be. Sometimes you can spot her only by the port wine noses of the gentlemen of her age about her. She is not averse to an occasional drop of the hard stuff herself. The lady, after all, is a Scot.

In her Castle of Mey, a piper wakes her. He chooses the tunes. She has to guess what they were. It's a great game.

She likes fun from the minute she wakes. (King Edward VIII said she brought into the family a lively and refreshing spirit and made family life – under King George V, remember – seem fun). How much of today's Royal Family life springs from her can only be a matter of conjecture, but it is certain that Prince Charles, who is very close to her, owes a lot of his sense of humour to his grandmother.

Thrust into royalty by the abdication, she had to do a lot of hand-waving from golden coaches and royal limousines.

If you are old enough to remember her lips moving, she wasn't saying, 'Thank you, thank you,' she was singing, 'Daisy, Daisy, give me your answer do…'

She is 71, Wullie. Yet she turns out for the annual parades of her regiments. She nips around by helicopter. When the Queen is abroad, she holds investitures, receives heads of missions, opens hospitals, goes to gala charity performances, and visits prize suburban gardens. But that's just the job itself.

The woman herself, when she sees a small boy struggling with the focus ring on his camera, will wait until he has got it, and his snapshot, right.

In Clarence House, the racing dowager has a bookmaker's 'blower' system installed to give her runners and prices at meetings all over the country.

She throws luncheon parties she doesn't let on about, for fear of upstaging those given by her daughter. At them, she brims over with unforced charm.

She is steady minded, and quite tough, like Willie Hamilton himself. She is also a sweet, serene, and beautiful grandmother with a bit of a glint in her eye.

So, come on, Willie.

What the hell do you want for your money?

Or, come to think of it, ours?

16 December 1971

But what does *she* think when meeting us?

THE QUEEN, to put it mildly, is slightly stunned and very happy. The cool, collected and highly professional monarch has been, in the language they use at the palace, 'completely taken aback' by the joy and affection showered on her in Scotland during the first of her summer-long progresses to meet her people.

Because royalty tries to think of everything, her 'Thank you' letters to the mayor of this and the chairman of that were planned even before she left London. By the time she returned over the weekend, it was obvious that they would not suffice, and there wouldn't be enough of them. Buckingham Palace secretaries are expecting overtime.

And what brought it about was not the State coaches and the jingling accoutrements and the jewelled finery. It was the fervour of the crowds who strained to touch her hand on her walkabouts, the people who burst out, as if she couldn't hear 'Oh, isn't she lovely?' or 'Oh, isn't she wee?' (She is 5ft. 4in.).

But surely, you may say, this was to be expected? Not exactly. Crowds can be capricious and, in the presence of royalty, curiously quiet. But not this year.

If Scotland is anything to go by, the Queen and the people are going to meet each other as never before. (Should you meet her, by the way, you address her as 'Ma'am.' If she proffers her hand, you take it, don't squeeze it).

It's the walkabouts, of course. It's a misnomer, I know, because I coined it in this connection. It was first tried, and has been mostly used, in New Zealand and Australia. Now it is to be used, not without some security misgivings, throughout the whole of Britain. It gives people their only chance to look directly into the Queen's violet blue eyes, to see the smile which lights her whole face.

It's not just us looking at her, remember. She's looking at us. Luckily for her, she is extremely shrewd. And she has a quite remarkable sense of humour.

There really is no need to tell her that your new sewage plant works on Guggenheim's double di-helix suspension principle because she will have read that up the night before. But if you go on and on about it, she has a smile that can stop you in mid-mumble. She doesn't mind a bit if the mayor drops the keys to the city. The people she mimics in private are the ones who have bored her. Like most clever women she is very interested by personalities, scarcely at all in local big-wiggery.

She can be disconcertingly forthright. One of our ambassadors, trying to explain a Middle East head of state, got into a hopeless whirl of circumlocution until the Queen rescued him by asking: 'Are you trying to tell me that the man is bonkers?'

At a rather grand reception in Brussels, I was missing from my appointed place when she bore down on our group. When she asked where I was one of my idiot colleagues blurted that I had slipped away to the bar.

'Yes,' she said. 'He would.'

She doesn't miss much. We once talked, in the royal yacht Britannia, then in harbour at Wellington, New Zealand, about a ludicrous local law which closed the pubs at 6 pm giving rise to a national high-speed jug-up known as 'the six o'clock swill'. She knew it well, for she had first proceeded through the streets as the pubs were closing. 'And some of the sights were *very* interesting indeed.' She said it with meaning and laughed out loud.

We all know how regal she can look. Indeed, at the beginning of her reign, she had the notion that she was somehow expected to look rather solemn in public. Also she was and to an extent still is, shy. But now she uses humour and curiously unexpected forthrightness as tools of her trade.

As Sir Harold Wilson told me: 'She has this ability – inherited from her mother, I think – of being able to put anybody at ease.' She sits for countless portraits – for regimental messes, high commissions abroad – and has a stock joke to put a new artist, in Buckingham Palace for the first time, at his ease. 'Now then,' she says as she enters, 'with teeth or without?'

CHAPTER FIVE

Her decision to travel Britain by train and royal yacht may have seemed curious at first. She is not passionate about trains. Nor is she a particularly good sailor. No, she is just being considerate.

Tradition would have demanded that she stay the night with the Lord Lieutenant of the county. And he, honourable old warrior though he be, might have had to stretch his overdraft to accommodate the royal party, let alone the risk of giving his cook-general the heebie-jeebies.

And anyway, in train and yacht, she can be sure of a supply of Dundee cake, shortbread and after-dinner mints which are a bit of a family failing. She can kick her shoes off (she always does), catch up on the latest news about horses, and go to bed with her own, special feather pillow.

She is enviably fit, eats sparingly, follows Weight-watchers, makes one glass of wine last a meal (though she can cope with a heavy snort), has a wonderful complexion, and can work a 15-hour day. It is difficult to see how she will ever work harder than during this, her Silver Jubilee year. It is, of course, important that she can.

In a curious way, the social function of the monarch is still her most important function. For she incorporates in her person the whole history, the sense of continuity of the nation.

She is not acting a part. Indeed, the idea repels her. The monarchy is one of very few human institutions which has remained constant – not by resisting change but by shifting subtly. The Queen has certainly changed. Her sanity, shrewdness, directness and humour make her very much the mistress of her times.

She is open to our scrutiny and criticism all her public life.

This summer will afford her the chance to have a closer look at us, without being able to publish her judgment. We will gawp and gaze and cheer and try to touch her hand, and mumble some banality when she tries to get a conversation going.

No matter. She knows.

She will be looking at people's eyes. Judging by Scotland's example she will like what she sees there.

We, in our turn, will see a figure who looks too frail to carry the weight of majesty. And women will say – they always do – that she's just like us, really. That is true. Except that, inside the nice woman is a proud Queen and a strong link in the chain of monarchy.

30 May 1977

VINCENT ON YORKSHIRE

If you've never heard of Morley, that suits us fine

WILL THE GOVERNMENT please take its filthy hands off Morley, which happens to be my home town? Morley, apart from producing Asquith, has never bothered the central Government, and I see no good reason why Whitehall should bother us.

If you have never heard of Morley, that suits us fine. We are a bit of a mucky 'oil in the Heavy Woollen District of the West Riding, and most of us know each other, and we'd like to keep it that way. We lie inside the Wakefield – Bradford – Leeds triangle, and we manage very nicely, thank you. As a parliamentary constituency we are linked with Batley, which is an even muckier 'oil about three fields away.

We don't reckon much to Batley folk. It's mutual, and we respect them for it.

We were here long before our mention in Doomsday Book. William the Conqueror had the neck to give us to one of his marauding Norman mates, one de Lacy, who had the gaul (forgive the pun) to rule us from Pontefract, of all places. Now we are about to be given away again. And I, and 40,000-odd others, object.

Bigger problems, at home and abroad, have tended to obscure the fact that home towns like mine are about to disappear under the Government's plan to restructure local government in England and Wales by the appropriate date of April 1,1974.

Where we come in, is as part of West Yorkshire, Area 6, District B (sounds like 1984 already, doesn't it?). We shall be as one with the rural districts of Wetherby, Tadcaster, Nidderdale and Wharfedale; the urban districts of Rothwell, Otley, Knaresborough, Horsforth, Garforth and Aireborough; the boroughs of Pudsey and Harrogate; and the county borough of Leeds.

That's the so-and-so. Leeds. Megalopolis. Already its tower flats are stalking like daleks towards the lower slopes of our hill town. They want to clear their slums (Morley is well ahead of them in that) and guess where they'd create new ones? That's right. Area 6, District B, once known as Morley. In a word, right on top of me. And I don't want them.

We shall lose our mayor and town council in exchange for a couple of seats or so in the chamber of the megalopolis. Oh, they will leave us certain local responsibilities for education and personal services. But as far as the town hall is concerned, we might as well offer it to a supermarket.

The Association of Municipal Corporations, representing more than 130 boroughs and county boroughs, says: 'The bigger areas now proposed can only mean less contact between the governed and the governing, and the taking of decisions by representatives inadequately aware of local circumstances.'

And so, in their various ways, said the townspeople who mounted the stage at the town hall here the other night.

It was perhaps a unique town meeting, politics out of the window and everybody's message 'We don't want to be swallowed up.'

The place was packed and they voted for an unheard-of referendum on the matter. Whether it will cause a tremor in Whitehall is doubtful, though if every town affected did the same it certainly would.

Dammit, we are about as far from Harrogate, in every way, as is Stepney from Weybridge. Who is going to make a viable whole out of such disparate places?

Local Government in England: Government Proposals for Reorganisation (Cmnd. 4584, Stationery Office, 12½p) sets out the proposals, but not the answers. Of the hundreds of towns affected, I can answer only for my own.

They're not daft. They recognise the need for local government reform, for the shifting of boundaries, and for a more equitable sharing of financial responsibilities. What the planners have taken little or no account of is local pride, even insupportable local vanity, which emerges even more strongly from the ordinary citizen than from the plump alderman with a bigger financial stake in the town.

If every town about to be affected, even destroyed, by the streamlining of the distant planners were to kick up as much fuss as Morley is about to, the Government would have a major problem on its hands. It has enough already. And the parish pump is not exactly a threatening weapon. Except that what comes out of it are votes.

15 September 1971

The great pie saga

FEW PROBLEMS facing rural England today equal the challenge the Yorkshire village of Denby Dale has taken up: How to cart a six-ton pie down the 1 in 8 gradient of Ranter's Hill without drowning the driver in 10 cwt of gravy.

They're going to bake this gurt good pie – the biggest in the world, naturally – up in Hector Buckley's barn. And between Hector's barn and 'the field' there are forces of gravity which might shoot the gravy – if not the meat-and-tatie monster itself – into the driver's left lug-'ole.

Denby Dale (pop 1,000) invites the engineers of the world to offer solutions. But not from London, please. Denby has *had* London. In 1887, Denby Dale, already feeling its oats as the mammoth pie centre of the world, let the thing go to its head so far as to invite a London maestro to orchestrate 1½ tons of beef, veal, lamb, pork, rabbits, hares, pigeons, grouse, ducks, plover, turkey, geese, suet and spuds into a symphony of a pie for Queen Victoria's Golden Jubilee.

And it stank.

Today, 77 years later, I was told with long-preserved bitterness: 'The chef smelled it on the eve of the big day and skipped off on the night train back to London.' The high pie is still up here in Toby Wood, buried in quicklime. And ever since only Denby Dalers have baked pies here.

The tradition of monster pies began in 1788, to celebrate – prematurely, as things turned out – the recovery of George III from mental illness. There's usually been a bit of bother ever since. One rose and got stuck in the oven.

The 1846 pie (repeal of the Corn Laws) slipped off the platform and was literally trampled to death by 15,000 pie-mad spectators. The last pie, belatedly celebrating, in 1928, the end of World War I, was consumed by as many of a crowd of 100,000 as could close with it.

Now, pie-mania has seized Denby Dale again. 'They've gone daft,' say the pie-less villagers around. Daft, in Yorkshire, is a word capable of infinite nuances. Denby Dale has gone admirably daft – but not gormless. The 1964 pie, which will meet its glorious fate next September, was conceived to celebrate nothing in particular. It has since come to be loyally, though vaguely, linked with the four royal births. But it has more to do with hilarity than heirs, more with booze than babies.

It is a lark, an almost forgotten species of village lark from another age – and it has inspired an incredible response of good will and practical help from hard-headed officialdom and big business. The NCB is said to have 'played hell' because the Yorkshire Electricity Board won the honour of cooking the monster. Six breweries fought for the concession to supply ale for the great day. Caterers, ice-cream manufacturers and fairground operators are still locked in battle for Denby Dale's favour.

A sheet metal firm has already made the pie dish – 18ft x 6ft x 20in. – and plans to sail it from the works at Otley to Leeds with a cocktail party aboard.

Denby Dale finds all this quite reasonable – a proper tribute to its pie. But even this imperturbable, implacably Yorkshire village is contemplating the day itself with some awe. They expect the biggest crowd to gather anywhere in Britain this year – all fighting for 30,000 portions of pie at half a crown a go for charity.

'There is no doubt,' says John Netherwood, printer, 'that this is going to be the biggest event in the country.'

One gets the impression that the pie committee, 100 strong, is already struggling to keep its monster in perspective. What started as a village lark has become something close to an obsession.

'It's a right clown of a village, this,' says Brian Kitson, the 39-year-old engineer who will be in charge of the pie's 18 cooks. I only wish we had more such clowns among our villages. Wise clowns, that is, who can get 10cwt of gravy down a hill.

And daft enough to get 250,000 people to pay for the privilege of just watching.

4 April 1964

The Yorkshire joke

THERE WAS THIS FELLER pulling a bit of string up Briggate, in Leeds. When this other feller asked him why he was pulling it, this feller said: 'Have you ever tried *pushing* it?' If you smiled at that, and you are a Southerner, you are eroding one of the North's most cherished beliefs – that Northern jokes, like Northern beer, don't travel much farther south than Sheffield.

The number of Northern comedians who are stars of TV and radio (I needn't go further than Morecambe and Wise) seem to give lie to Yorkshire's claim. But it is important to distinguish the comedian from the *joke*. A classic Yorkshire joke is the one about Enoch coming into the parlour where his old friend, Joe, is laid out awaiting the undertaker.

'Well, Ah'll be beggared,' says Enoch, 'Ee does look well.' Says the widow: 'So he should. We'd just come back from a fortnight in Bridlington.'

Now that *is* Yorkshire. I take it from a slim, and probably contentious volume called *Austin Mitchell's Yorkshire Jokes*. Yorkshire Television claim the copyright on these Yorkshire jokes (and I wish them the best of luck).

As I come from a Yorkshire wapentake much older, according to Doomsday Book, than Leeds, I feel I am in a position to confirm that people do say, of a corpse: 'Ee, doesn't he look lovely? Doesn't he look like himself?' (Who the hell do they imagine he *would* look like?). But when you live in a two-up and two-down, with a shared lavatory across the yard, you might be forgiven for forgetting the natural phenomenon; all corpses shed years in looks.

There are still parts of the mucky West Riding where black humour is strong meat. 'Well,' they say, 'you have to be able to laugh to live round here.' It is both stoic, and a cry of despair.

I hold it to be a plain and self-evident fact that there is no such thing as a 'British' sense of humour. There may be common themes, such as understatement and a preoccupation with sex and lavatories, but we are too tribal to share all jokes.

We Yorkshiremen are, in a sense, the Texans of Britain – though we prefer to think of *them* as the Yorkshiremen of the US. (Our feelings towards, or against, the tribe across the Pennines, are a private affair, and both of us would be glad if you'd keep your hands off.)

VINCENT ON YORKSHIRE

I agree with the author when he claims: 'We keep our laughter for the really important things in life: death, disease, and defeats at cricket.' I've heard lots of mucky tales in Yorkshire. Indeed, I am something of a connoisseur. I hear very few 'dirty' stories there.

Take the one about the old Dalesman given a council flat. His friend, Joe, asked what he was going to do with his pig.

'I'm taking him with me.'

'But where are you going to put him?'

'I'm going to put him in the bedroom.'

'But what about the smell?'

'Chuff smell, pig'll soon get used to it.'

There is a blissful belief in Yorkshire that urban Southerners cannot appreciate such humour, with its emphasis on grit, doggedness and an exclusively Yorkshire refusal to be surprised at whatever knocks nature can dish out.

I shall devote the rest of my space to what I consider to be the definitive Yorkshire story.

When the old man won a quarter of a million on the pools, his friends asked: 'What are you going to do with the money, Harry?' He pointed out that he'd never even been out of the village in his entire life (you can still find them), and meant to take one of these round-the-world cruises he'd read about, to think it all over.

The travel agent, with a pile of tickets a foot high, was very patient. Harry had to be outside the working men's club at the crossroads at 7 am. When the Number Five bus came along the top ticket would take him *all* the way to Bradford. He'd be dropped at Central Station, where a fellow at a kind of gate affair would take the second ticket, which would take him *all* the way to Liverpool. Then on to the first of the cruise ships. There was the ticket, the berth, the cabin number, and so on, all the way round the world.

It went perfectly as far as Liverpool, where Harry boarded the Mersey ferry. Five minutes later he was landing at Birkenhead, with a bloke at the bottom of the gangway shouting: 'Tickets, please,' Harry, with his little 'tache case and his big pile of tickets, asked: 'Which ticket do you want, then, young man?'

The scouse eyed the pile of tickets and asked: 'Where the hell have you come from?' At which old Harry grabbed the foreigner's lapels and snarled: 'Great Britain – the finest country in the world.'

That's Yorkshire.

26 June 1971

VINCENT ON IRELAND

How I didn't quite marry Princess Grace

IN THIS HISTORIC, if slightly squelchy, sod in County Mayo the Mulchrones and the Kellys are shortly to get together again. For my part, it should have happened years ago. Unfortunately, Prince Rainier saw Grace Kelly first. Things might have been different had it not been for two restless young men who emigrated from these parts about 80 years ago. One was Princess Grace's grandfather. The other was mine.

And today I treated myself to a daydream – a pastime not at all frowned on around here – about what might have happened if they'd both stayed put. I was lying in the long grass beside a little lake they call 'The Leg of Mutton' – possibly because it looks nothing like one. Below me was the cottage John Kelly, Grace's grandfather, left to seek his fortune in America. From its doorway you can see, across the water, the house where the Mulchrones still live.

So Grace and I could have been neighbours. We could have gone to school together, walked home together down the green boreen. I would have carried her satchel, naturally, and Cupid could have taken it from there.

Ah, if it hadn't been for John Kelly and my grandfather. And Prince Rainier. And my wife.

But now Her Serene Highness is coming back to where, for the two of us, it all (almost) began. I beat her to it by a few weeks. It will be her first time here. This is mine. And I only hope she has better luck sorting out her relatives than I had across the lake.

Her relatives, in fact, are currently doing their own sorting, indulging in a fierce sort of blood sport to separate the second cousins (who will be presented to her) from the less favoured Kellys. As there are about 50,000 Kellys in Ireland – only the Murphys are more numerous – I wish them the luck of it. (There are only a few dozen of us Mulchrones, yet at the end of just one day's genealogical inquiries I was sneaking a look at my driving licence to make sure who I was.)

Princess Grace is not going to escape this sort of Mulchrone mist, for the simple reason that the old Kelly cottage is now occupied by one of us. Mrs Ellen Mulchrone, silver-haired and ruddy-cheeked, wears hobnailed boots on her feet and the names of her more obliging saints (Bridget and Anthony) on her lips.

I wanted to talk about Grace Kelly. She wanted to talk about the Mulchrones. She won. A dozen times at least she started scrambling up the family tree. 'No, if you're Paddy's son, and his father was Charlie, wouldn't that make you a second cousin to the Mulchrone that went to Philadelphia...?'

That was about as far as we ever got. It was far enough, anyway, to convince the hospitable widow that I was of her kin, and to be made welcome. 'The neighbours are coming in to clean up the old place before Grace comes,' she said. The cottage is about 200 years old – thatch showing through the roof beams, stone floor, harness on one wall, coloured prints of the saints on another, a rosary hanging familiarly at the side of the open hearth.

Mrs Mulchrone has lived in the Kelly cottage since she married, 42 years ago this weekend. And it was before that, she confided, 'that a gipsy told me a beautiful woman would visit me from Europe, and the diamonds hanging from her. But never mind that now. Are you sure that tea's strong enough?' The brew was strong enough to fell any one of the widow's 12 cows, but I managed to get out that it was fine.

From hand to hand the Mulchrones passed me on, using a dark brown liquid to do a sort of litmus paper test on me to see exactly what I was made of. Late tonight they found out I'm not a Mulchrone at all. Or, rather, I'm a Mulchrone from another branch of the clan who never were neighbours of the Kellys. I must have looked crestfallen. 'Well,' they hospitably conceded, 'maybe you're a sort of second cousin, once or twice removed.'

So we left it at that. I don't really know whether I could hang around to help welcome Her Serene Highness on the strength of being a second cousin, once or twice removed, of the people who used to live across 'The Leg of Mutton' from her grandfather. I mean, I wouldn't want her to think that I was trying to get in on the act.

27 May 1961

The Kennedys who stayed and the Kennedy who returned

One of the despatches which won Mulchrone his award as Descriptive Writer of the Year.

WELL, THERE WAS SODA BREAD and apple pie and sponge cake and open flans, wheaten bread and wee buns, free beer and tea you could have stood a spoon up in. There were roses and carnations, and lilies and ferns – all in silver pots and all sitting on the farmyard floor (concreted by orders from 'them').

There were 46 policemen before you even began counting their officers. There were photographers from Pittsburgh shooting from the byres and worried looking fellahs from Washington hovering around the phone marked 'White House' stuck on an old table in the lean-to where the Ryans hang their harness.

There was the schoolmaster and 40 shy kids, the doctor and the parish priest and his two curates, and suspicious buffs whose civvies shrieked Dublin Castle. There were American colonels biting the tips off cigars, just like they do in the fillums, and American corporals doing the same, and isn't democracy just great.

The whole townland and countryside was out in the gear it bought for Whitsun, charming its way through security lines laid down by the White House itself. And all this in the Ryans' little farmyard where the biggest recorded crowd to date had been eight. And seven of them cows.

Oh, yes, and there was the President of the United States. A darlin' man, no doubt, but he didn't get much of a chance to shine at the loveliest, most loving, daffiest, daftest, tea party in the history of Dunganstown, County Wexford. Or anywhere else for that matter.

'Welcome home, Mr President,' said the banner over the old boreen, though Mr Kennedy might be excused for thinking that home was never like this.

All the women neighbours were in to help lay the trestle tables in the farmyard. The finest linen in the neighbourhood graced them, but the wind and the rain (it was what the Irish tend to call 'a lovely soft day') threatened to ruin the spread. So all the next-best linen was impressed to be laid over the cakes and scones and the wheaten bread, and pinned down with drawing pins. And when they ran out of drawing pins they improvised with stones, daintily wrapped in paper napkins.

And when eight helicopters landed in the fields behind the house, blowing a whirlwind of dust over the scene of the feast, at least one of its founders said a word which we are all glad the President didn't hear.

The moment produced its cynics, of course, like the one who said (in a reasonably cleaned up version): 'Sure, isn't civilisation funny? We used to eat inside and go to the toilet in the yard, but now we eat in the yard and go to the toilet inside.' But this is put down as sheer jealousy at the fact that the Ryan home sprouted a toilet and bathroom especially for the – well, for the convenience of the guests who stayed 45 minutes.

Mrs Mary Ryan herself, the President's 63-year-old second cousin once removed – plump, motherly, but with a wary eye – was in her new dark blue floral. Daughter Jose, 25 and the image of a younger President Kennedy, had been up as usual at six o'clock to see to the cows.

Now she had her pearls on. Sister Mary Anne, 22, a nurse up in Dublin, wore a gold choker and a bouffant hair-do.

Lined up stiffly behind them stood Mrs Ryan's brother, Mr James Kennedy, who has acquired a golden tie clip in the shape of the President's wartime PT boat, and his grown children, Patrick, Peggy and Kitty and a married daughter, Mrs Anna Rowe. Jose blushed prettily and diverted the

President's attention to sister Mary Anne, who greeted him with the assurance of a girl from the big city.

By now the presidential party was swarming into the farmyard, which was beginning to look like a rush-hour platform at Waterloo.

If for no better reason than that the farmyard was by now uncomfortably crowded the President edged his way in to the Ryan farmhouse. They all stood, or sat, like the still eye of the milling, shouting, storm which was the farmyard when the smiling, open-armed President stepped from his car into Mrs Ryan's fond embrace.

'I'm glad to see you,' he said. 'Sorry for all the trouble we've caused you.' With a gracious sweep of her plump arm Mrs Ryan dismissed the eyes, ears and top security men of the world from her thoughts. The President turned to Jose, whose very teeth are extraordinarily like his. 'You were a very tiny thing when I was here in 1947,' he said.

He passed – indeed, he did not even trouble to inspect – the forlorn little outhouse which local legend says is all that remains of the homestead from which his great-grandfather, Patrick, left for America in the post-famine years.

In the newly painted farmhouse Mr Kennedy greeted all his cousins again in private, adding an invitation to Mrs Ryan and her two daughters to visit him. Mrs Ryan said later: 'We shall be going in the near future. We shall be staying in the family home, of course. Yes, certainly, I mean the White House.'

Cousin Mary Anne poured President Kennedy a cup of tea, with cream and two lumps, and he nibbled a piece of wheaten bread. He also tried a sandwich filled with salmon caught by cousin James. He laughingly agreed to cut one of the two iced cakes baked by neighbours – the one which bore 'a plaque' of his head in pink icing. He drove the knife into his own left ear.

The President raised his cup of Mrs Ryan's tea (her recipe is 'Keep it strong') and said: 'I raise my cup of tea to all the Kennedys who went and all the Kennedys who stayed.'

Then he looked around the tables and asked: 'What are you going to do with all this food?' – but decided on the family's behalf to offer it to the Press. It was well meant, but the Press and police took him so literally that there was nothing left for the schoolchildren, who had been expecting a tuck-in.

A last fond squeeze of Mrs Ryan's hand and he was airborne in his helicopter. Press and security men made a dash for the 100 or so cars which they had left at the direction of the police in an adjoining field. But when they tried to drive out of the field they found their way barred.

The guardian of the gate said: 'My name is Tom Rowe. Yes, I'm related to the President, and it'll cost you five bob to get out of here.' And it did.

For one of the Kennedys at least America is not the only land of opportunity.

28 June 1963

It's King Vincent from now on

THE OYSTER FESTIVAL starts in Galway, tomorrow. But for the moment I am cold sober. I want that clearly understood before I tell you how I became King of Ireland.

I have been reigning now since breakfast time. I suppose I owe it to history to record that the accession took place somewhere between the kippers and the toast. It was then that the Professor of Early Irish, at University College, Galway, said quite distinctly: 'There is no shadow of doubt that you are descended from Laoire, who was king of Ireland when St. Patrick arrived.'

I took it quite calmly, really. But then, I've always known that I was – well, different. My friends remark on it frequently, though in rather more vulgar terms.

I shall count it *lèse-majesté* if you commoners smile at the news that the Professor of Early Irish is a Miss Kathleen Mulchrone. The professor (no relation) is a witty woman, but she does not joke about early Irish history. In fact, her 'period' stops at the 12th century, and she gives the impression that she hasn't a lot of use for anything that has happened since. Her wit is at its most biting on the subject of those tourists who hunt their Irish genealogy. The Irish, never loath to turn an honest dollar, have learned to keep a straight face when Hiram P Hackensacker comes over and announces that he is a descendant of Brian Boru. They congratulate him on his good fortune and sell him his family crest.

Professor Mulchrone never researched our name, though it is a very unusual one, even in Ireland. But when working on early manuscripts clues began to fall into place. And that led to the discovery that the blood royal flows through the veins of you-know-who. She kept this news to herself. 'If I told them at the university,' she said with a wicked smile, 'they'd lock me up.'

I have no such inhibition. It is just a question now of how to break it to Ireland, which has had its share of trouble, heaven knows, that it's King Vincent the First from now on. I mean, how are three million Republicans going to react to a king with a Yorkshire accent?

The Oyster Festival might be my time to strike. By this time tomorrow night 1,000 dozen Galway Bay oysters will have slid down the throats of the citizenry, and they'll be in no fit state to resist my claim. Some people say it is the best party in Ireland, which is to say a lot. Oysters are only the excuse. They come from as far as Munich for the singing and dancing. One group of determined party-goers is coming all the way from Cleveland, Ohio.

Nobody expects to get much sleep tomorrow night. The morning after is catered for, too, with a massive Irish coffee party. It was added to the programme a few years ago out of sheer thoughtfulness for the departing guests. It has remained for a slightly different reason. The organisers found that people who had booked out of their hotels tended to book back in again (perhaps a little unsteadily) as soon as the coffee party was over.

Perhaps it has something to do with Danny Lydon. Danny, the wine expert at the Great Southern Hotel, burns a little whiskey in the glass before pouring in more whiskey and the coffee. His art has made him famous all over the world.

'The Irish coffee king!' they call him.

Of course, they'll have to stop that when I take over. We can't have everybody getting into the act now, can we?

25 September 1965

Where time was made for man – and talk

IN THE PAST COUPLE OF HOURS I have seen one motor car, three swallows and a swishing swan. (You know the sound their wings make.) And more beauty than I can drink in. The next parish behind me is Boston, US. The Atlantic has washed the wind. Before me – Roaring Water Bay, the Fastnet Light, and the islands where they speak the old tongue.

I remember Tim the Caper – for he was Tim from the island called Cape Clear – when first he caught sight of a visitor wearing contact lenses, quietly asking a fellow Irish-speaker, 'What name has the little man with the scale of the bream in his eye?'

When the tide slackens I think I'll go down to the rocks to prise off some mussels with my knife and we'll have *moules marinieres* for lunch. This for me is the good life. I have breakfasted on eggs Benedict and Bloody Marys on a Sausalito balcony overlooking San Francisco Bay, and dined on sucking pig baked in an earthen trench on an island off Fiji. But here is where I want to be. This is the last 'undiscovered' coastline of Europe. I want a cottage here, a small stake in its life, its beauty, its ineffable peace.

The English – the more discerning among them, I'd like to think – are coming back here to stay. As old Tom-Tom (ie, Tom, son of Tom) said the other day: 'Jaysus, it took us 700 years to get the English out, and now you're buying it back from us.' Why? Well, because we've had enough of packaged tours and the crowded Mediterranean. We can put up with the 'lovely soft days' – an Irish euphemism for rain coming down like stair-rods.

Ireland has over 2,000 miles of coastline. You go find your own bit. Mine, only three hours from London, is where the bare, granite bones of the land surface from the soft green of the picture postcards and grope in splendid headlands into the Atlantic.

I can fish for free. I can pick all the cockles and winkles I can eat. I can shoot my own lobster pots. I can get crab for practically nothing, plaice for a little more, smoked salmon for half the London price. I have eggs laid this morning, ham from pigs I have known, chickens that never saw a battery. I can get soda bread, wheaten bread, potato bread and barm brack. 'Do you want your bread warm, or will this morning's do?'

The hills play their tricks with colours, a fresh palette daily, but always ending with the misty purple which Coco Chanel once told me inspired so many of her creations. The gorse is custard yellow just now, but soon the stunted tropical palms will begin to sprout, and foxglove and honeysuckle will border your travelling until the fuchsia falls from the massive hedgerows to roll a red carpet before you.

Much of the land is barren and rocky, and ruined cottages remind you how life drained away with the haemorrhage of emigration. There was a toast written in those times which went: 'Health and long life to you; land without rent to you; a child every year to you – and may you die in Ireland.' The last I would happily do, for it has given me so much of the good life. Not just it, but they, the Irish. I write, in spite of my name, as a Yorkshireman.

Some can't abide the Irish, whom they consider feckless, fey, and ignorant. I'm sure some of them must be. But they are also brave and gay and un-material still, and their saints and scholars, having first Christianised a bit of England, went on to teach at the Court of Charlemagne. (They also gave us whiskey. Any letters to the contrary from Scotsmen will go straight into my fire.)

One fall-out from the older, calmer culture is a deep abiding courtesy – an honest, caring kindness which envelops the sweet-sad land, and the stranger. Strangers on the road raise a hand to every passing car. After a while the English find themselves doing it to each other. When did *you* last raise one hand from the wheel and salute a passer-by, just for the love of your fellow man?

If you think of it as John Bull's backyard, don't come. This is a foreign, Celtic country whose warmth, especially towards the quiet, friendly English, will disconcert and seduce you.

A fighting Irish pub is largely a fiction. The sound of a pub in the West of Ireland is a low susurration of voices discussing the price of heifers. Until, at night, somebody might start a ballad session in which the illegitimate birth, and fiery fate, of the Black and Tans might well feature. Usually they will take pains beforehand to explain that they don't mean you. You will rarely hear a swear word, if only because the children are there. It's illegal, but they're there, and welcome. None of your leaving them outside with a coke and a packet of crisps. It arises partly from the fact that most pubs double as grocers' shops – and occasionally as undertakers – and children run errands. Aspirins, son? Ah, there they are, on the top shelf, between the ubiquitous statuette of the Infant Jesus of Prague and the box of stuff that's for collywobbles in cows. Will you have a lemonade while you're here? (And we think we are civilised.)

The village has 80 people and three pubs, an Irish equation I have never been able to work out. Of the 80, one was a Protestant. Until she died, last year, the rest took it in turns to give her a lift to Matins. The North? History's to blame. Not you.

Here, time was made for man, and talk. They prize it highly. By comparison, the chat in an English pub is small beer indeed. At noon, a man in the bar (he was in his pyjamas, but it would never have occurred to anyone to be so impolite as to ask why) was talking about somebody's poteen. 'After a sup of that,' he said, 'you could have operated on me and I'd have cheered ye on.'

To buy your way into this very special happiness is no longer cheap. Thirteen years ago, a friend of mine bought a two-bedroom cottage in the village for £200 – furniture thrown in. Ten years ago you could have bought half an acre, with a view over the bay, for £50, and put an excellent, pre-fab bungalow on it for £2,350. The situation now bears some comparison with the Cote d'Azur where, with prices on the shore gone mad, some people had the foresight to build in the hills about Grasse.

Another friend, a dentist, has done just that here – 10 acres in the hills at £50 an acre, and an old cottage thrown in which he is working on. But, as a local solicitor tells me: 'The Englishman's desire for elbow room, for landscape, and especially for seascape, is what has driven prices up.'

I know what he means. Planning permission is tight. The Irish, very sensibly, won't let you build on the seaward side of a coast road. My heart's desire, a view from a stoutly built, three-bedroom cottage on a third of an acre, will cost me about £6,000. Rates – perhaps £75. But the opportunities are limitless. Here, a bare hilltop acre for £1,000, though you'd have to bore for water. There, an old, four-bedroom cottage with a fabulous view over the sea. Yours for £4,000, though you'd have to replace the old roof for a start. Locally, they call it all 'the gold rush' and privately wonder why the English are so attracted. It's the peace. It's a way and pace of life the rat race will not touch in our time. It has a price beyond the reach of many. But for others, as they discover this glorious land each year, it is the place where civilised man can realise the good life. I really can't afford it. I truly can't afford to miss it.

8 May 1971

THE ESSENTIAL MULCHRONE

Forty yesterday and what I make of it

I DON'T MIND BEING FAT. And even less the fact that I'm unfit. But I hate like hell being 40. Which I have been now for one whole day. I'm sitting here, a fat, 40-year-old fool, watching a fold in the flesh on the back of my hand which refuses to go down.

Only a 40-year-old would be daft enough to chance his arm in one of those tests proposed by the more idiot magazines. You know the kind of thing: 'Are you a Sex Bomb?' 'Would you know how to behave at the Palace?' Well, I've locked the office door to try one called 'You get a little younger each day.' I'm on the 'How young is your skin?' bit.

'Lay your hand limply on a table,' it says. At 40 that's no challenge at all. 'Pinch the skin on the back of this hand between two fingers. Then release it. If the skin snaps back like a rubber band, take a bow for youth. Old skin goes back slowly.'

They might have put that bit first. Mine hasn't gone back *yet.* Can you sue people for this kind of irresponsible journalism? The stripling who wrote this nonsense says that a 40-year-old should be able to run a mile in exactly eight minutes. Anybody who knows me is aware that it takes me eight minutes to get from the office door to the nearest bar, which is exactly 85½ steps distant. I'm not even going to try the part which suggests that, at 40, I should be able to hold my breath for 23 seconds. And this, mind you, after jogging along at about 180 steps a minute for two minutes. (I haven't jogged along that fast since the day a Japanese tried to prevent me reaching even my 25th birthday.)

I remember the horror of the stocktaking which is forced upon one at 30. Well, at 40, let me warn my younger readers, the balance sheet becomes easy pickings for the Fraud Squad. How can this flabby, 40-year-old husk still house the nervous doubts I first recognised at the age of 16? I don't know how, but it does. And all the little achievements along the way, all the peaks of life so unscalable when dimly seen from the third row of the Speech Day choir – why have they left a taste of ashes? Is this *all* there is to it?

Physically, the signs are as obvious as they are depressing. Secretaries are no longer wary. The woman alone in the railway compartment no longer shifts uncomfortably at one's entrance. Rather does she welcome the appearance of a neuter St George to give battle to the imagined Teddy Boys due to involve her in some horrific Hitchcock situation beyond Surbiton.

Air hostesses instinctively know that it's a drink you want much more than a date at the other end of the line. And at a certain kind of Press party they steer you past the young ladies euphemistically called 'assistants' and straight to the refreshments.

I haven't yet had a younger man give up his seat for me. In fact I propose to thump the first one who tries. But I've had the chilling experience of joining a group of youngsters at a party, only to hear their irreverent laughter dry up as they sought to adjust their conversation to someone *older*.

It's one surrender after another. To my tailor, who has finally convinced me that braces are the finest invention since the disappearance of waistlines. To my wife, who, hearing from a dubious friend that an ordinary towel no longer meets the contingency between the locker-room and the golf club shower, now considerately packs a bath towel, 6ft long.

I'm suddenly at the age when not merely policemen but police inspectors are younger than I am.

When young men (39 or younger) presume to express opinions about things I know nothing about I don't exactly say 'Pshaw,' because I'm saving that for when I am 50. But I do find my face setting into that patronising 'if only you really knew' sort of mould which I find so depressing in 41-year-olds and over.

Oh, I suppose it has its compensations. I feel I can speak without being spoken to. I can talk arrant nonsense to wine waiters and school children and get away with it simply on account of my age. I can make a fool of myself, or be made a fool of, without minding very much.

I can... well...I'm sure there are lots more, anyway. It's just that I can't think of them at the moment. If you can, perhaps you'd let me know. But not, of your charity, if you're under 40.

27 September 1965

The second half of my life

IT IS MY FIRM INTENTION, some time during the second half of my life, to do something about the wonky handle on the sitting-room door. For a while it was possible to say to visitors who found it came away in their hands: 'Oh, yes, it came loose the other day, and I haven't got around to doing it yet.' But all the people who ever come to us have been back two or three or more times since then. And now they all know. It's not merely lack of opportunity, or even mere idleness. It's sloth.

It is the seventh of the seven deadly sins, and I commit it daily. The paint on the house moulders like my intellect, yet I do nothing to rejuvenate either. The gap in the garden fence grows like the gap in my moral defences, yet I plug neither.

The opposite virtues to the seven deadly sins (should you have forgotten them for the moment) are humility, liberality, chastity, meekness, temperance, brotherly love and diligence. And I can't remember when last I *unconsciously* practised any of them. (I have the notion that to practise any of them consciously is to cancel out the good in them and revert to the first and worst of the deadly sins – pride.)

Taking stock, any shopkeeper will tell you, is murder. Taking stock of your own life is like a taste of suicide. If I am not exactly sin-ridden, I am certainly guilt-ridden. Not oppressively so, or I'd open the window and jump. (The current oppressiveness may be attributable to an excess of hock at lunch – gluttony, or DS No. 5).

But I have been looking at the credit balance and find it woefully short. I am in terror that the first unselfish thing I can remember doing might also prove to be the last. It consisted of selling ha'penny milk tickets for Spanish Republican babies. It was being a Young Communist that made me do it, and I went in some terror that the Pope might find out that one of his lads in the West Riding was putting milk down the wrong throats.

Before becoming a reporter I was several socially acceptable things. I was a Bairn (of the Boots for the Bairns Fund), a patrol leader, an RAF pilot, a second-row forward, a sucker for 'fear God, honour the Queen, shoot straight and keep clean.'

And I can match most of your comings and goings, chum. I have eaten the finest meal in the world, flown an aeroplane, tried reefers, seen the sun rise over Everest and men die at the barricades. I have made and taken life, scored a winning try, made a Queen laugh and a child cry.

And what am I? I am a portly, winded, over-dressed, overfed, day-dreaming coward; a tireless, tiring juvenile; a hack with a small reputation for humanity which is, in reality, a calculated insurance against the rigours of the hereafter.

And me only half-way through!

When I was less than a quarter of the way through, and already shouting against the wind, I vowed that, when *I* was fat and 40, I would pay heed to any idealistic 17-year-old who told *me* how the world should be run. Well, any 17-year-old who presumes to say 'I think...' in my hearing is likely to qualify for the old thin-lipped, indulgent smile, and a reply in the order of 'Yerse, I remember Mr Nehru telling me...' Yet some of the ideals remain – an end to class and racial barriers, realistic pensions, the abolition of the death penalty, harsher sentences (perversely, perhaps) for cruelty to children, and an England free of the hypocrisy, cant and smugness which is holding her back.

I have longed, and almost invariably failed, to add my jot to international understanding. I tried it, in a small way, when reporting President Kennedy's recent visit to Ireland. (I am a Yorkshireman as a result of the Irish Famine, and believe, with Sydney Smith, that 'the moment the very name of Ireland is mentioned the English seem to bid adieu to common feeling, common prudence and common sense, and to act with the barbarity of tyrants and the fatuity of idiots.')

And what happened? I got a letter from the vice-president of a Hollywood movie corporation saying he thought my stuff 'one of the most, perceptive, humorful and scintillating pieces of reporting I have read in many, many years.' I was attacked by columnist Lord Arran for being too pro-Irish. And several Irish readers cancelled their subscription to the paper because they thought I was being too anti.

Given the chance, I will write columns about quiet, kindly, sensitive Americans as far removed from the common, grotesque image they have abroad as the Englishman is from his own image beyond our shores. I need columns because I can't say anything shortly. Perhaps it is smug, but I recognise the limitation. Forty is a good age for saying 'I can't...' with regret, perhaps, but without envy.

At 40 I can say to a younger man: 'No, thanks, I think I've had enough.' (I hope he thinks I'm being mature in my drinking. The truth is, of course, that I can't take as much as I used to. But at least I know it.)

I don't mind my shape on a beach any more. I used to look like the weed in the Charles Atlas advert, the one who had sand kicked in his eyes. Now I look like a pear. And I don't give a damn. (I pull the tum in when there's a blonde about, but then, who doesn't?)

I am several things I pity – a wine snob (in a cunning, deprecating sort of way), a dodger of responsibilities, a fool with money, a hearty teller of dirty stories, a snob about some things and an inverse snob to the point of ingratiation with taxi-drivers, waiters and porters, and those people who come to the door to change your religion.

I dislike myself most of all when I find myself in full 'father-knows-best' spate with my children. And when I am in my leave-me-alone mood and give a curt 'No' to their offer of a game of ludo, I recognise in their eyes a hurt I dimly remember. Then, ashamed, I play ludo. But why didn't I play in the first place?

And how, at 40, can I still go to sleep with a bitter husband-and-wife quarrel unresolved? 'We'll never sleep on a quarrel,' we said. Perhaps you made the same rule. Then why do I still break it? It is sheer, gagging pride, of course. The silence is torture to the soul. The making up is sweet indeed, but, oh, the pity of the lost hours. This surely can't, mustn't be allowed to go on for another half a lifetime. Halfway through, surely, I should be balanced enough to see short temper coming and step smartly out of its path. It is one of those little-big things which I now know to be more important than the grander ambitions of youth.

Cry shame, if you care, but I no longer want to save the world. The Mitty dreams are less and less frequent (I haven't saved England in years). I no longer want to upset the order of things – only to rattle it like a box of dominoes now and again.

The Tories give me a pain right up my left leg, and the present Labour bunch another all the way down the right. The Liberals come somewhere in between.

If only they would stop killing and maiming and prodding one another with electric cattle-probes I'd love the entire yewman race. I've seen a hell of a lot of it, and it's not a bad bunch when you get to know it. One of its favourite members will always remain – me. And I don't intend to do badly by myself. I've had the running, thrusting years, and a precious thin layer of knowledge and understanding and sophistication they have laid on me.

But I have another half to go, and a fair idea of how to occupy it. I would like to fill the second half with loving and ideas, and experiences and things I was in too much of a hurry to catch hold of back there in the thrusting 30s.

Having always shied away from the absolute truth about myself, I think I'll have a crack at learning a bit more about me. (Perhaps I'll wind up looking at a face like the hungover loon I sometimes see in the bathroom mirror, and then I'll wish I hadn't.) I'll do all the things I have regretted never doing. I'll learn how to sail a boat, how to build a wall. I'll buy all of Beethoven and read all of Dickens. I'll learn about flowers and to curb snide remarks. I'll not fly into a rage when somebody holds his knife and fork the 'wrong' way. I'll go to old pubs and listen to old people. I'll switch off that damned box in the corner, and I'll *talk.*

But, chief above all, I will try to understand what being a husband and father is about. And I will try to perform that most glorious of all man's earthly tasks as diligently and as cheerfully as my nature will allow. This I must do. This, in the second half of my life, I will do. Just as soon as I've fixed the handle on that damned door.

17 September 1963

Happiness

HAPPINESS is being left a million quid in somebody's will. For me that is. You please yourself. You can plump for your first cuckoos or your last rose of summer, your walking barefoot on hot sand or cool grass. Every man to his own happiness.

Me, I'll take the money.

Until it actually arrives I am making do quite nicely with present happinesses, which include bread and jam sandwiches, folded over, and a quarter of liquorice allsorts with lots of black ones.

JB Priestley is very good about happiness, which he sees as a great blue bubble which suddenly floats up, unbidden, and without human control. 'When you expect it,' he tells me, 'it doesn't come. I remember once walking to a London bookshop in a blizzard. It was a foul day, yet the bubble floated up, and with it came the most glorious happiness.

'You know the thing in the United States Constitution – the one about life, liberty and the pursuit of happiness? Well, the Americans have been miserable ever since. Because you can't pursue happiness. You just have to wait until the bubble comes.'

For me the bubble floats up every time I cross Waterloo Bridge. I can summon the bubble like a genie simply by sitting on the top of a bus, looking at London, and saying to myself: 'I'm going to *do* you.'

Happiness is playing rugby, squash or golf, and holding on to the thirst until after the shower. It is also the relief of taking off a pair of gumboots. It is being reintroduced, by children, to 'sweet' tobacco, aniseed balls and sherbet fountains. How long since you ate a jelly baby *limb by limb?*

Happiness is the adolescent realisation that acne is receding and a beard beginning.

It is fish and chips out of the paper and a pint of bitter with a handle on the glass though only in Yorkshire. It is being jerked awake at dawn by a two-year-old devilish angel who has two fingers in your nostrils and is pleading, over and over, 'Cuppertea, Daddy...'

It is also finding a forgotten ten-bob note in your breast pocket, and hearing ice tinkle in a glass. It is the sound of oncoming bagpipes, and being married to a woman whose first choice is the montelimar.

It is being miserable at coming to the end of a good book and then discovering it is one of a series – remember your first taste of *Just William, The Saint,* the Peter Cheyney books, John Masters, Laurence Durrell? It is all of Mozart and some of Beethoven, and all you can remember of the songs your mother used to sing.

It is a quarter of champagne, frozen almost stiff, and drunk at exactly 10 am. It is some kinds of wine, and all kinds of candlelight. It is wood smoke and deep-pile carpets, a new handkerchief and the smell of leather.

Happiness is your gratitude for one or other of God's gifts.

And until that million comes along, I'll be happy with all He gives me for free.

24 December 1962

World Cup or World War?

Occasion: the morning of the final of the World Cup, July 30, 1966 – the one that England won.

IF THE GERMANS beat us at our national game today, we can always console ourselves with the fact that we have twice beaten them at theirs. And how's that for narrow, nationalistic hedging from one who has never in his life paid as much as half a dollar to watch 22 men disputing possession of the hide of a cow?

I speak as a unit of Soccer's lost millions. Or, rather, as one who was never tempted to the terraces. I played Rugby – the game which doesn't go in for kissing the scorer. (When you can't get to kiss him, if I can believe my TV screen, you now jump on him – constructing a sort of vertical, alley-cock-a-lorum phallic victory symbol in the middle of the field while the fans bay their pleasure.)

You may have hated the World Cup, as I think I did, but you couldn't ignore it. It has encroached more deeply into the inward-looking British temperament than any international event since the one we now know as the second world war. Indeed, it has *been* war. And a very valuable little war, too, if only because it showed us how nationalism can raise its idiot cry over a cowhide. And I'm not thinking of foreigners hanging trainers in effigy, or quaking Latin trainers suddenly finding they have urgent business in the Outer Hebrides. I mean us.

The World Cup emptied the pubs. (And you're a fool if you skip over that statement without savouring all its horror.) Housewives went all Greer Garson on us and stood shoulder to shoulder with us before the idiot box. Our children, who were being brought up as woolly minded internationalists, now whip out nasty little toy pistols at a mention of Argentina. When the evening matches were on, the suburbs cringed under a deathly hush. Gardeners froze over their hoes, like the people in *The Angelus,* except that they were listening to their neighbours' radios and their prayers were that Eusebio wouldn't do it.

We have sub-editors in this office whose only reaction to the Last Trump would be finding a headline to fit. Yet they sat transfixed at their desks, half stoned out of their Rule Britannia minds at the news coming through their transistor earplugs.

'Eng-*land,* Eng-*land,*' cried Wembley. And I'm sure it's silly to hear echoes of 'Sieg *Heil!* or 'Ban-*zai*'.' But hysterical triumph in a crowd is much the same no matter what the cause, and I didn't like the sound. They were not, I repeat, defending a freedom, they were kicking a cow.

I have been consoling myself with readings from the works of the football writers, a body of men rising magnificently to their moment. Theirs is a sub-division of English as rich and as distinctive as pidgin or Bombay Welsh. Even when employed on the Rovers v Wanderers on a wet Wednesday in West Hartlepool it is the most jingoistic tongue we still dare use, every adverb at attention, every adjective at the salute. Well, after that semi-final, they broke and unashamedly wept. They begged heaven to witness that there had been only eight fouls. Had there ever *been* such a clean game in Soccer's temple? Had life ever tasted so good?

Win or lose, tomorrow's papers are going to be sheer hell. The shame of a defeat will be exceeded only by the horrors attendant on a victory. The deductions that will be drawn about the future of the British nation are already terrifying. And what bothers me is – how the hell did I get mixed up in it?

30 July 1966

Just guess whose wobbly bath has missed the census...

YOU'D BE SURPRISED what an awful sense of loss it gives you. Not having one, that is. A census form. It's all right for you, because you've done yours and probably had it collected. You're safe. You're free, white, 21, and a bit of a national statistic. I, on the other hand, am in a kind of

State limbo. I didn't even get a form. The Government doesn't know to this moment whether or not I have a fixed bath. (As a matter of fact I have a fixed one which wobbles when you get in or out, though I imagine the nation can rub along without that information.)

To tell the truth, when the forms were distributed I was cruising the Shannon with my gunnels awash with Guinness and thinking of other things. But I came home dutifully, before midnight last Sunday, to fill in the form. I had a vision of a pretty enumerator calling at one minute past midnight to pick up the form and check on who was sleeping in the place.

I hear some people don't want to answer some of the questions. I, on the other hand, will answer anything. If only I had the blasted form. How can I escape the £50 fine if they won't give me the form? There was a moment of panic when I imagined that they thought me of no account and didn't want to know about me. But I put that aside. According to pub talk, which is all I have to go on, they want to know about everybody.

The difficulty lies in *what* they want to know, and the answers are very difficult to find in pubs. With the £50 fine very much in mind I would like to assure the Government that the Mulchrone household has no secrets. If, that is, it knew the questions. I have asked all my friends, and the only one who could remember said they wanted to know 'How do you and your household occupy your accommodation?'

The only honest answer to that is that we occupy it in a state of barely controlled mutual belligerency, though I doubt if that is what the State wants to know.

Short of the actual form, I can only offer the census people the answers to such questions as my friends can only vaguely remember. How many rooms? Eight. Ages? I was 48 yesterday. My sons, including the two in Yorkshire, are 15, 14 and ten. My wife tells lies. I can't be more honest than that.

There's a quaint question, it appears (don't forget this is all new to me) about flush toilets with the entrance outside. Well, the truth is that the ten-year-old is still agile enough to make it through the downstairs lavatory window when we've locked ourselves out. Again, I can't tell whether this is going to help the country until I've seen the form. Anyway, the downstairs one is really out of bounds when we are using the hall as a dining room. Does the census form rise to such subtleties, one wonders?

And is it true that they ask 'How many hours per week does that person actually work in the job?' Because if so I am going to find my pen hovering a bit. May one count the time spent thinking, straightening paper clips, gazing at the clouds, replacing leads in propelling pencils of fiendish complexity, taking the necessary pills, rifling through old files, and re-balancing loads of old, but possibly vital, bumph in their mesh trays? If I walk three paces to the window and look down into the street in search of an adjective, is that work? If I listen to a bore in a pub in the hope that he will come up with a gem of information, which part of the time spent could be called work?

It's not knowing what they want to know that's making me nervous. Surely they don't want to leave me out altogether? The awful discovery is that if there is one thing worse than being a bit of a statistic, it's not being part of the statistic at all.

24 April 1971

All's well darling... but how I wish you were here

IT WAS ABOUT THREE days after my wife left me that the washing machine started to follow me across the kitchen floor. I do believe it thought I was trying to feed it. It was juddering with excitement, slavering suds all over the place, and its little wheels were pointing straight at me. So I pulled out its plug. Dammit, a man's got to be the master in his own house.

When the wife's away, that is. Mine took the kids away on holiday three weeks ahead of me. What's left of me follows in a few days' time.

Take sardine tins. Did you know that that little opener-thing opens them only half-way nowadays, leaving you poking with a fork for the rest of the mush? Before I leave tins (not that, for the past three weeks I have left them for a moment) I suggest that, by law, a first aid box should be attached to every kitchen door.

Then there's ironing boards. It's shameful that a country which invented the Industrial Revolution hasn't yet come up with a method to iron the shoulders of a shirt without impressing an irremovable pleat on the front, where it shows. And when the fold-up clothes prop slipped leaving my damp shirt cuffs dancing all over the yard, I felt my nerve slipping with it.

It wasn't supposed to be like this at all. Like all married men, I've been a bachelor. Don't worry about me, I said, as they drove off. (I'll even admit it now, in my broken state, to having had dreams of nights out with the lads. I was even looking forward to the minor pleasures of totally undisturbed evenings with books, with a glass ready in hand.) The cruel truth was that, along with the papers, she'd stopped the order to the wine merchant. Have you ever tried tinned rissoles with a choice of tonic water or ginger ale?

There were four rissoles in the tin, a delectable dish for two according to the label. Forgetting the fridge, I ate all four, and felt bloated for days. I consulted a confirmed bachelor. 'You buy the biggest tin of beans,' he said, 'use what you want, and the rest will keep in the fridge for up to a fortnight.'

He omitted to tell me that you have to take the residue out of the tin, and put them in a plastic whatnot. When next I felt an urge for beans, I had a very healthy penicillin mould. The bread went green overnight. Mind you, it had been in the bin a week or more. And a boiled egg without bread is, well, quite distinctive.

Don't they make tinned steak and kidney pie for one? Or pud? Who caters for the loners of this country, that's what I'd like to know. Not my supermarket, anyway.

I've tried to follow her disciplines, like washing up immediately. Hands that have never done dishes now feel as soft as my face – with a day's stubble. I've made my bed every morning. A quick smoothover, and a little tuck in. Trouble was, there were so many tucks that the sheet threatened to disappear entirely beneath the mattress and I had to start all over again.

I reassure myself nightly that empty houses are supposed to make noises, but mine creaks and groans like that phantom ship, the Marie Celeste. Could it be settling, imperceptibly, into the lush green marshlands of Surrey, and me with it? Perhaps I should pen a last message and lash it to the TV aerial.

The new, plastic, water tank split the day the bill arrived and turned one wall of the small bedroom into the consistency of cold porridge. I rang the plumber. He said he had a slipped disc. (Memo to self: Never again upbraid wife for pleading with plumbers rather than shouting and bawling threats down telephones like a true-born Briton.)

As the days wear on, I am more and more grateful just to find myself alive. I find myself talking back to the people on the radio, grateful that there are people somewhere out there.

She took the car, so I walk to the station hating other people's impeccable gardens. (Usually I get half way down the drive until, assailed by doubts, I turn back to check that all the windows are closed and that I haven't left a cigarette burning on the edge of the bath.)

There's still a pack of snails for four and a tin of chilli beans in the larder. All's well darling. Don't worry. I'll be with you soon.

7 August 1972

O death where is thy sting-a-ling-a-ling

THE FIRST BRIBE I ever took as a reporter was half-a-crown. I was seventeen, and he was dead. 'Would you like to have a look at him?' the widow asked. Office instructions on the point were explicit. I looked. The other women in the little West Riding kitchen gathered round as the handkerchief was lifted from his face for the umpteenth time. He was my first corpse, and for the first time I heard what was to become a familiar litany – 'Ee, doesn't he look lovely...? Better in death than in life, Sarah Jane... Doesn't he look like himself?'

I was backing out when the widow reached under the tea caddy on the mantelpiece and handed me the half-dollar. I composed my pimply features and explained that there was no fee. This, I said, was journalism. But I must take it. *He* had left it for me. But he didn't know me. She knew that. 'Before he died,' she explained, 'he said "When I've gone, they'll be sending somebody round from t'*Observer*. Tell him to have a pint wi' me – and tell him to get t'bloody thing right".'

By chance I came across his funeral tea. They were burying him with ham at the Co-op Hall. There was tea – great, steaming, practically untouched urns of it. The Co-op was run by Primmers, but the janitor wasn't one, and winked an eye at the bottles smuggled in from the pub over the road. The therapy stopped short of a knees-up. But I've been to worse *parties.*

The feast was splendid. The widow, who conceded that I'd 'got it right,' explained that, as well as the insurance, she'd had him in a club. There are still scores of burial clubs listed with the Registrar of Friendly Societies, survivors of hundreds started in Lancashire early in the nineteenth century to avoid a pauper's grave and provide a bit of a do for the mourners. The Friendly Funeral Society, founded 1815, offered the relatives a benefit of *48s.* – and 2s. more 'provided they have beer to the amount of 4s. where the collecting box is.' The link between pubs and funerals is an old one.

A funeral used to be an occasion, sometimes grand, sometimes boozy, generally a great display but always, one might almost say, full of life. Corpses were always 'beautiful', funerals always 'lovely'. Now it's twenty-five minutes at the crematorium (and a 'fine' if the clergyman runs over time), a peek at the flowers on the way to the gate, and a cup of tea in the parlour. Where we used to see them off with ham, now we do it with high speed gas. An ad in the funeral trade press says, 'High Speed Gas – chosen by over ninety-six per cent of Britain's crematoria.' Where, one wonders, are the leisurely four per cent?

A man used to lie in his own church and be buried in his own churchyard. Now the body goes to a 'chapel of rest' and its disposal becomes an embarrassing sanitary exercise set to Muzak.

Well, say the undertakers – 3,500 of them run a £60 million-a-year industry – we offer chapels of rest because vicars can't afford to heat churches for just a few hours. And because so many families are out of touch with the church the undertakers frequently hire a clergyman most mourners have never seen before and may never see again. He will officiate for as little as a guinea. The only briefing he needs if the crematorium, too, is strange, is on the location of the button that will send old Fred sliding Stage Right to the Gas Board's special pride.

Occasionally the dead themselves insist on paying for a last round for the boys from the coffin. An old Yorkshireman recently left instructions for his cortege to stop outside the George and Dragon, where he had left a fiver for the purpose. Said his son, 'As he was a happy man who looked on this as his last joke, we played it out.'

Andre Simon, the wine writer, ordered champagne for his memorial service. A Cheshire publisher arranged his own funeral stag party. His son said, 'Father had a wonderful sense of humour.' Old men, you see, with a glint in their eye, and memories of funerals as they used to be.

You don't get the racy funerals of old any more. It's ten years now since Johnny 'Scarface' Carter, Sid the Con, Nick the Ape and Freddy the Fly were at a funeral together down Camberwell way. The deceased was a motor trader whose £6,000 Cadillac crashed in flames near Tower Bridge, and so many of the lads turned out that the cortege stretched for a mile. The best wreath, by general consent, was a four-foot billiard table with six legs of red carnations, a green moss surface, and a set of ivory balls and a cue. Lovely funeral.

There can be happy affairs. I was at Pandit Nehru's funeral along with about half a million others, and that was quite a gay scene, with vendors selling chapattis and pop in the crowd. They watched his body pass and smiled fondly because they do not make our mistake of equating the corpse with the life that was in it. There was no hush. How could there be, when everybody wanted to say goodbye.

The English scoff at the Irish wake, not appreciating that it has nothing to do with dogma or superstition, and very little (apart from a prayer or two) with the corpse, but a great deal to do with sustaining and cheering the living. I survived one in West Cork earlier this year. Then his friends, as is the pleasant custom, dug the old sailor's grave, but not too deep, for they soon struck another coffin. He barely got below ground, and in the hush a voice said, 'Jaysus, he hasn't got six inches of freeboard.' Everybody smiled. Why wouldn't they? They loved him.

Our funerals have become mean, miserable, embarrassing affairs with, at crematoria, as much style as a production line. Dammit, the Chinese hire men to bang gongs and carry crazy floats. We go with a hum of tyres and a hiss of gas. Taped music, an optional extra, is used for solace the way the big jets use it just before landing.

When I go, give me a Basin Street funeral band, Belgian black horses with plumes, a stop at the tap room of The Hermit, and lots of ham. It won't bother me, mate. But it might just take that miserable look off *your* face.

Reproduced by kind courtesy of **Punch**
30 December 1970

And now...
'Let's be kind
to me' day

LONG BEFORE THE FLOWER PEOPLE cottoned on to it, a friend of mine conceived a simple way of obliging everybody to be nice to him. About once a year he would declare 'This is "Let's-be-nice-to-Rodney day",' just like that. And, do you know, people were so taken aback that they were.

His wife and kids pandered to his whims. His friends, stunned by his effrontery, which was quite unshakeable, bought him drinks, deferred to his opinions, even opened doors for him. The following day he would be as miserable as you and me. But, by God, he enjoyed himself on the day itself.

There's a crying, national need for such a day. It would do a lot to restore the status of the birthday, perhaps. Or one could declare it any old time, when the mood was low.

Right. Tomorrow is 'Let's-be-nice-to-Vincent day.'

Let's see. I want bitterly cold orange juice, crisp bacon and fluffy scrambled eggs. I want my toast hot from the toaster, and I'll put my own butter on, thank you very much. Nobody ever puts the right amount of butter on my toast.

I need at least an hour in the bathroom, and the razor blade must have been used just once before. (It beats me why the manufacturers don't use them once before they dish them out, because new ones are murderous.) I want Jack de Manio to be a bit hung-over and getting the time wrong. The weather outside will be crisp and sunny, and my suit will have just come back from the cleaners. But before I put it on I want nine holes of golf, and the sight of sleepy squirrels and dopey, envious commuters passing the 16th in steamed-up trains.

The morning post will have no bills, no letters from the bank, the Inland Revenue, the council or the man who has bought my name and address and now tries to make me feel inadequate for not buying encyclopaedias, deep-freeze foods and courses in Russian.

I shall have lost my cough, and I shall run up the stairs in the bus. The bus will be on time. So will the train, the tea in the office, the morning paper and the post. The porter will be the Ukrainian one who still likes people and actually says 'Good morning.' My shoes will be highly polished, though comfortably cracked, like an old man's face.

I shall lunch at the Vendome on Prawns Walewska and a glass of Chablis. And even so, somebody during the day will say: 'Are you losing weight?' My second chin will not make a greasy mess of my tie knot which, in turn, will not slip, unnoticed, three inches down my shirt front.

My wife will ring to say that, unlike the traditional British craftsmen who traditionally overcharged for not curing the damp chimney breast in the bedroom, the latest has fixed it for a reasonable sum. I shall admire a mini-bird's thighs, and she'll see me doing it, and she'll laugh with the enjoyment of being admired instead of giving me that dirty-old-man look. (I mean, where, in the name of all that's hopelessly lustful, are you supposed to look?) My kids will all score tries. Tries cost me half-a-crown a time, but I reckon they're worth it.

I want crackling, clear sunlight the whole visible length of the Thames, from Westminster to St Paul's, when I cross Waterloo Bridge. I want Norman Shrapnel in good form in *The Guardian.* I want the latest editions of *Punch* and the *New Statesman,* and the latest book by Leslie Thomas.

I want a quarter of a pound of Riley's Chocolate Toffee Rolls. I want an old friend to ring me, preferably from Yorkshire, to talk about nothing in particular, unless it's to offer me a ticket for a Rugby international.

The boss will say: 'You mustn't overdo it. Why don't you get home early?' A taxi will swing in the second I raise my hand. My wife will have descended from her Cordon Bleu mist to make Irish stew, the kind you eat with a spoon. And there'll be a bottle of young Beaujolais, about two months old. (If the Beaujolais you're drinking has a year on it, you shouldn't be drinking it.)

There'd be Morecambe and Wise on television. Then the loveliest music in the world on the record player – it's called *Miserere* – but by now I'm too far gone in euphoria to explain what it is.

Then, for a liqueur, a thimbleful of straight malt whisky, preferably the pale, smooth water of life called Glenmorangie. Then you may shoot me. For I shall have had my day.

15 December 1969

Lightning Source UK Ltd.
Milton Keynes UK
UKOW052240271112

202852UK00016B/1042/P